Money
Creation and Evolution
Temptation

David C. Cook Publishing Co.
Elgin, Illinois / Weston, Ontario

Hot Topics Youth Electives: Money, Creation and Evolution, and Temptation
© 1990 David C. Cook Publishing Co.
All rights reserved. Except for the reproducible Student Sheets, which may be copied for ministry use, no part of this book may be reproduced or used in any form without the written permission of the publisher, unless otherwise noted in the text.
Scripture quotations are from the *Holy Bible: New International Version* (NIV), © 1973, 1978, 1984 by the New York International Bible Society. Used by permission of Zondervan Bible Publishers.
Published by David C. Cook Publishing Co.
850 N. Grove Ave., Elgin, IL 60120
Cable address: DCCOOK
Designed by Randy Maid
Illustrated by John Duckworth and Randy Maid
Photo by Bill Bilsley
Printed in U.S.A.
ISBN: 1-55513-206-5

CONTENTS

What's So Hot about Hot Topics?

Let's face it: You want the kids in your youth group or Sunday School class to *like* you. Sure, you want to be respected, but you want to be liked, too—at least a little.

That's why you cringe when you're called upon to teach or lead a session on a topic you know your kids will hate—say, Sibbecai the Hushathite in I Chronicles. You know you'll have to dress up that topic with funny hats, run relay races around it, and serve banana splits afterward just to keep kids from using that dreaded word—*boring*—about you.

It doesn't seem fair, does it? You do all that work, and kids turn up their noses just because they can't instantly relate to the topic.

You deserve a break. That's why we created Hot Topics Youth Electives.

Hot Sessions

First, we picked the subjects most kids are already concerned about—things like money, dating, drugs and alcohol, and careers. That's so you can announce, "Hey, kids—next week we're going to talk about money!" Sounds better than Sibbecai the Hushathite any day, doesn't it?

Then we got some of the country's most experienced writers of youth programming to come up with sessions that explore those hot topics. We gave those writers a challenge: to create sessions that were full of creative activities *and* substantial Bible content. Each session would have to be usable in Sunday School *and* youth group, aimed at high schoolers but adaptable to junior high. Preparation would have to be easy, too—no forcing the leader to collect 300 bottle caps, two films, and an armadillo to do the session.

It was a tall order, but they did it.

Hot Tips

Next we contacted some of the most respected youth workers and speakers around—people like Josh McDowell, Jim Burns, and Barry St. Clair. We asked them to tell you how to approach these hot topics with your kids. We told them to think of themselves as friendly advisors sitting across the kitchen table from you. The resulting how-to articles would help you get ready for each unit of sessions.

That was a tall order, too—but they came through with flying colors.

Hot Format

There was still one thing left to do. We had to make sure each book was easy to follow. So we clearly marked each session's aim, key verses, and materials at the start (we called them The Point, The Passages, and The Preparation). We gave every step in the session a title and goal of its own. We put instructions to you in regular type, things you might say to kids in bold type, and suggested answers in parentheses.

We also put reproducible student sheets at the end of each unit of sessions. That's so you don't have to buy separate student books or worksheets.

Have It Your Way!

These sessions aren't just hot. They're flexible. They're active enough for youth group meetings and retreats, biblical enough for Sunday School. You can use this book in all sorts of ways. For instance:

• Use it for a 13-week quarter, leading the 12 regular sessions and one of the bonus sessions.

• Use it for a month at a time, working your way through a topic for four or five weeks.

• Use single sessions whenever you need them.

In other words, you can use them any time you want to get kids talking about—and applying biblical principles to—their favorite subjects.

Do that, and you may become one of their favorite leaders. And next time you have to talk about Sibbecai the Hushathite, they may even listen.

Have a hot time with these topics!

—John Duckworth, Editor

How to Talk to Kids about Money

by Jim Burns

A few months ago I decided to tackle the subject of money and stewardship with our youth group at church. Honestly, I had no idea what to expect. I started our time with a simple discussion starter: "Let's go around the living room and share what we want to be when we grow up."

Derek was first. He said, "I want to be rich."

I said, "Okay, but what do you want to do to become rich?"

He shot back, "I don't really care what I do; I just want to make a lot of money, live by the ocean, and drive a Porsche."

At first I thought Derek was kidding. But I seemed to be the only one in our group of eight who was amused by his comment. All the other students took his statement at face value.

Another young man in the group said he wanted to be an entrepreneur. Again I laughed, but he was serious. I didn't know what an entrepreneur *was* when I was in high school—and I still can't spell it without the help of a dictionary.

Most of the other students gave more typical answers like doctor, nurse, and professional baseball player. It dawned on me that most of the kids wanted to make a lot of money and, in a real sense, thought money would be their ticket to the good life.

Now, I am not opposed to money or even the necessary pursuit of money. Unfortunately, though, the kids in your group and mine have accepted many myths about this potentially explosive subject that may hinder their spiritual growth and development.

Money Matters

Finances are not a peripheral issue in our faith. Jesus spent more time talking about money than He did about love. He was talking about faith and commitment when He said, "For where your treasure is, there your heart will be also" (Matthew 6:21).

Unfortunately, the kids we work with are bringing to the group a great many mixed messages and a lot of cultural baggage when it comes to the subject of money. In a not-so-subtle manner, the culture blares at them, "The person with the most toys wins," "Look out for number one," "Who says

success is not spelled M-O-N-E-Y?" And the list goes on.

With a more subtle approach kids are bombarded by the clever consumerism of this generation. Today's young person believes that if he or she wears the right clothes, buys the perfect car, or purchases the best of whatever, he or she will be truly happy. Our generation equates happiness with things.

One youth worker put it this way: "The dominant spirituality of this generation is the spirituality of consumerism." Kids believe if you can buy "it," chew "it," drive "it," consume "it," then "it" will make you happy. A few years ago on television sets all over America we heard, "Buy a Chevy, drive a Chevy, live a new Chevy." How do we "live" a new Chevy? Somehow, mysteriously, most of our kids believe deep in their hearts that money will bring them happiness.

Unfortunately, many of the kids we work with will miss the true meaning of stewardship, vocation, relationships, and giving. Like their families before them, they will try to serve God *and* money even when Jesus is very clear on the subject:

"No one can serve two masters. Either he will hate the one and love the other, or he will be devoted to the one and despise the other. You cannot serve both God and Money" (Matthew 6:24).

Living in a Material World

The practical issue we must deal with is this: How do we help our students live in a material world and remain faithful followers of Jesus Christ?

Is it easy? No.

It is possible? Yes.

Here are a few suggestions:

1. *Teach Stewardship as a Holistic Approach to Discipleship.*

If someone wants to follow Jesus and be His disciple, it must involve his or her time, talent, and treasure. Rather than saving that message for the yearly church fund drive, we should place it as the central issue of commitment to Christ. I am convinced that we have used the "soft sell" approach with kids for too long. They deserve the right to know at a young age that if they are going to be

Christ's disciples they will need to give Him their finances as well as time and talents.

2. *Teach Responsible Financial Actions.*

There is a large group of people in our country who spend more than they make. Thousands of marriages break up because of this, and faith is compromised—not to mention the near majority of people whose hearts have been broken by irresponsible financial behavior.

You have chosen to lead sessions that are literally central to your students' faith and happiness. You can prevent a great deal of hurt and future turmoil by teaching financial responsibility now—before your kids make costly mistakes.

3. *Teach the Biblical Command to Help the Poor and Oppressed.*

When we brought Jennifer back from a week-long mission trip to a poverty-stricken village in Mexico, she told her dad, "We aren't middle class; we're rich."

When kids' hearts are broken by the things that break the heart of God, kids are moved to commitment. This means they need to see need; then they will respond financially.

Jesus said, "From everyone who has been given much, much will be demanded" (Luke 12:48). Practically speaking, along with leading these sessions on money, you may want to sponsor as a group a child from a Christian relief agency like Compassion International or World Vision. When you give your kids the opportunity to give financially, they will be able to experience a new depth to their commitment to Christ.

A Rare Opportunity

As you begin these sessions on money, you have a great opportunity to prevent your students from making some of the same mistakes some of their families have made. I look at teaching kids about money like this: Imagine a high cliff with a long, dangerous drop. You have the rare opportunity of building a fence at the top of the cliff and preventing your kids from having to pick themselves up at the bottom because of costly mistakes.

When you talk to kids about money, talk to them as straightforwardly as you possibly can. And remember, how we deal with our money is a central issue in our Christian commitment.

Jim Burns is a veteran youth worker, author, and national workshop leader. He directs the National Institute of Youth Ministry in San Clemente, California. His books include The Youth Builder *(Harvest House Publishers).*

MONEY

by Steve Rabey

Steve Rabey is a writer who lives in Colorado Springs. He is a former editor for Compassion International. His books include *Rock the Planet*, a collection of devotions for young people (Zondervan, 1989).

Money is one of those subjects you're not supposed to discuss in public.

But that didn't stop Jesus. According to Richard Foster, author of *Money, Sex, and Power* (Harper and Row, 1985), "Jesus spoke about money more frequently than any other subject except the kingdom of God."

Money—and how we relate to it—is central to the way we live. It's also become a major issue for many teenagers, whose interest in making "the big bucks" seems to have skyrocketed during the last decade.

Whether they're planning ways to make money or just spend it, your young people are interested in the subject. They need to hear what God says about it—and they aren't going to get a godly perspective from slick and skillful advertisers. Nor will they hear it in much pop music, which often has espoused anti-biblical positions on money—from the Beatles, who sang, "Give me money, that's all I want," to Madonna, who proclaimed, "I'm a material girl."

This session is designed to help your kids start taking a good, hard look at money and materialism. By leading, you can help kids begin to develop healthy, biblical approaches to stewardship that can guide them for the rest of their lives.

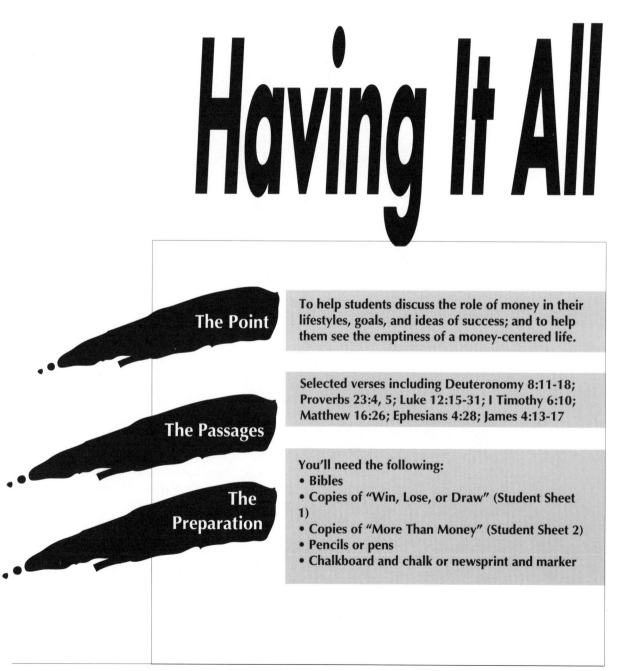

Having It All

The Point

To help students discuss the role of money in their lifestyles, goals, and ideas of success; and to help them see the emptiness of a money-centered life.

The Passages

Selected verses including Deuteronomy 8:11-18; Proverbs 23:4, 5; Luke 12:15-31; I Timothy 6:10; Matthew 16:26; Ephesians 4:28; James 4:13-17

The Preparation

You'll need the following:
• Bibles
• Copies of "Win, Lose, or Draw" (Student Sheet 1)
• Copies of "More Than Money" (Student Sheet 2)
• Pencils or pens
• Chalkboard and chalk or newsprint and marker

6-12-96
WED-

I Want It All!
Talking about Our Appetite for Money and Things

Seat the group in a circle if possible. Have the student to your right finish the sentence, "I want a . . ." The next person to the right repeats that sentence, then adds another item he or she wants. The process continues around the circle, with each person repeating all the previous items and adding another.

Keep track of all the items on a list of your own. Any student who can't name all the items in order and add another is "out." Keep going until nobody can remember the whole "wish list," or until it's time to move on to the next part of the meeting.

Sounds like we want a lot of things! How much do you think our whole wish list would cost?

What effect do you think having all those things would have on you?

Explain that a lot of people today, kids and adults, say they "want it all." In this session you're going to talk about what that means—and whether it's really worth wanting.

How Do You Spell Success?
Comparing Financial and Other Kinds of Success

Pass out copies of "Win, Lose, or Draw" (Student Sheet 1). Ask kids to fill these out individually. Encourage kids to express their real opinions in their answers. Then discuss:

How did you decide who the winners and losers are?

Answers will probably capsulize kids' definitions of success. Write key phrases from these definitions on the board or newsprint, paying special attention to the role money plays in the definitions.

Which people couldn't you classify?

If kids think about it, they may see that most of the people can't be classified—especially with so little information to go on. A rich person could be unhappy; a person on welfare could be successful as a friend; a person who reads the Bible daily might not practice its principles; a disabled person could be a successful student, parent, worker, etc.

If having lots of money doesn't guarantee success, why do you think so many people try to make a lot of money?

How do the kids you know try to make money? What do they do when they get it?

What do you think a Christian's attitude toward money should be?

Battle of the Bucks
Understanding Some Biblical Principles about Money

Form four teams, each to study one of the following passages. After a few minutes, regather the whole group and discuss. Ask each team questions like these:

*Group 1—*I Timothy 6:10

Is money the root of all evil? (It's when people *love* money that they get in trouble. That love can overpower other loves, including love for God.)

What does it mean when it says people have "wandered from the faith

and pierced themselves with many griefs"? **Where did these people go, and how did they "pierce" themselves?** (They let their love for money and the things money can buy grow in importance until these things were more important to them than their faith in God.)

What "griefs" come from loving money today? (Getting arrested for stealing, worrying about your wealth, spending all your time making money, etc.)

Group 2—Deuteronomy 8:11-18

What do these verses warn against? (Letting your heart become proud and forgetting God.)

How could that happen? (By loving your wealth so much that you forget God gave it to you; thinking you could produce it without Him.)

Money doesn't just drop out of the sky. How can we say God gives it to us? (He gives the ability to earn wealth.)

Group 3—Luke 12:15-21

What is Jesus getting at? What does a person's life consist of? (Our lives should consist of spiritual wealth, through our relationship to God, with physical wealth being of less importance.)

What makes the rich fool foolish? (He thought life is made up of things instead of relationships with God [or people]. He thought plenty of good things were all he needed, and that once he had them he could dedicate his time and energy just to having fun.)

How does one grow rich toward God? Does God have some kind of bank that we can store money in? (We grow rich toward God by being humble, following His will, obeying His written commands as well as His tugs on our hearts, and in not putting physical things ahead of spiritual things.)

Group 4—Luke 12:22-31

What is it about the birds and lilies that Jesus likes so much? (They don't fret or worry about their daily needs. People, on the other hand, worry and fret and get ulcers and have heart attacks. God wants us to be more like the birds and lilies.)

Verses 22-31 tell us not to worry. Does that mean we shouldn't work or earn and save money? (The point of the passage is in the final verse: Put God first and the rest of life will work itself out better than if you put possessions and riches first.)

What "things" will be added to us if we seek God's kingdom? (The things we actually need—not just things we want.)

Then address this question to the whole group: **Based on these three passages, would you say money is more like a hungry tiger, a workhorse, or a pet hamster?**

Answers will vary. Point out that these verses concentrate on the dangerous, tiger-like side of money, the side that threatens to pull us away from God. The temptation to love and serve money and possessions is probably too strong to compare it to a pet, but money can be a "workhorse" when we put it to good use instead of letting it use us.

Your Financial Future
Seeing How Our Attitudes Toward Money Affect Our Goals

Have kids look at Student Sheet 1 again, calling their attention to Persons B, C, G, and H. **Would you want the jobs these people have? Why or why not?**

How important do you think money is in choosing a job or career?
Pass out copies of Student Sheet 2, "More than Money." Help students

put salaries in perspective by helping them fill out the sheet. You might get the ball rolling by giving your answers to the first job, "Sunday School Teacher or Youth Worker." Your ratings might look like this: Earnings, 0; personal satisfaction, 10; service to people, 10; service to God, 10.

You may need to help students with general salary ranges. After the sheets are completed, discuss:

Which jobs got the highest overall scores? Which got the lowest?

Are there jobs that pay little financially but offer high rewards in all three other areas?

How would you rank the four categories in order of importance?

Have one student read Proverbs 23:4, 5, and another read Ephesians 4:28.

What do these verses have to say about making "big bucks" the top goal for your future? (Money isn't worth wearing yourself out for, because it's gone before you know it; we should work so that we have money to share with others who are in need.)

Having It All (Almost)
Seeing the Emptiness of the Money-Centered Life

Get one or two responses to each of the following questions:

What are you planning to do today (or tonight) after you leave this group?

What are you going to do tomorrow?

Do you have any plans for next week?

What about next month or next year?

Read James 4:13-17, about planning, making money, and boasting.

Does God want you to sit around and not make any plans? What's the point of this passage? (God doesn't want us to plan Him out of our lives, as if we can make money and do other things without His help. Planning is okay, even necessary. But while making our plans we should retain our humility and keep our eyes and ears open to God in case there's something He wants us to do.)

Read Matthew 16:26, about gaining the world and losing one's soul.

How much money do you think there is in the whole world? Let kids guess.

Why is one soul worth more than all that money? (Your soul lasts forever; money and the things it buys will eventually disappear.)

If time allows, discuss people in the news (embezzlers, frauds, inside stock traders, errant TV evangelists, etc.) who have allegedly done something wrong in order to get money. Emphasize that most of us are tempted, too, to let money run—and ruin—our lives in some way.

Close in silent prayer, asking kids to tell God about their view of "having it all."

Our Bibles, sermons, hymns, and prayers are full of the word *Lord.* All this talk about the lordship of Christ sounds fine—until we come to the subject of money.

"Sure, Christ is Lord," some adults insist. "But when Jesus said that stuff about giving away your money to the poor, or the rich person not going through the eye of the needle, He was just speaking figuratively!" Is it any wonder so many kids grow up thinking that their use of money is none of God's business?

The testimony of the Bible remains clear: Christ wants to be Lord of every part of our lives. This session introduces kids to the idea that our use of money is indeed "His business."

None of His Business?

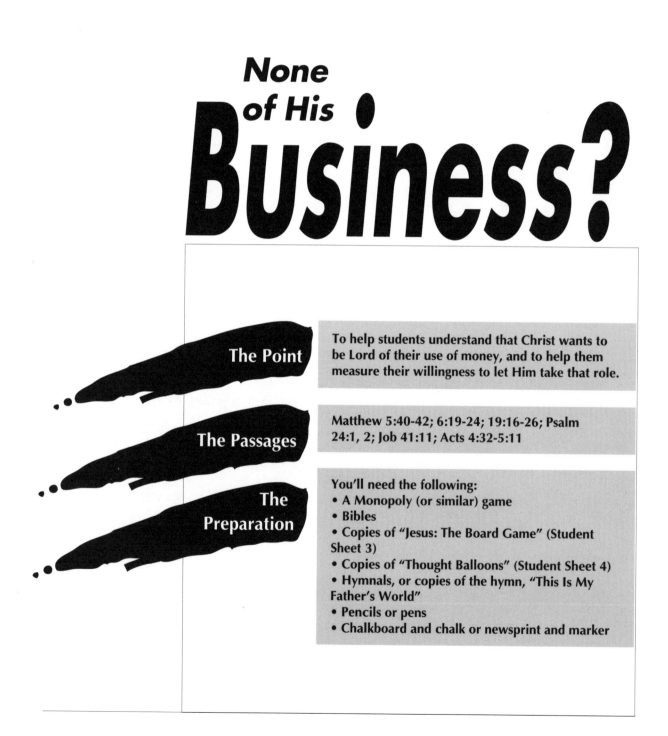

The Point

To help students understand that Christ wants to be Lord of their use of money, and to help them measure their willingness to let Him take that role.

The Passages

Matthew 5:40-42; 6:19-24; 19:16-26; Psalm 24:1, 2; Job 41:11; Acts 4:32-5:11

The Preparation

You'll need the following:
• A Monopoly (or similar) game
• Bibles
• Copies of "Jesus: The Board Game" (Student Sheet 3)
• Copies of "Thought Balloons" (Student Sheet 4)
• Hymnals, or copies of the hymn, "This Is My Father's World"
• Pencils or pens
• Chalkboard and chalk or newsprint and marker

Jesus: The Board Game
Contrasting the World's View of Money with That of Jesus

Step 1

Bring a Monopoly game (or a similar game that emphasizes accumulating wealth) and display its board, game pieces, play money, etc. to the group. Explain, or ask a student to explain, the game's objective. If time allows, have a few students demonstrate by playing the game for a few minutes.

Monopoly isn't the only game that concentrates on making a lot of money. "Trump: The Game" was the name of a board game based on the reputation of multimillionaire Donald Trump, a tycoon famous for owning real estate, airlines, and other properties. The purpose of the game was to work your way around the board, capturing as many properties as possible, increasing their value, and selling them at a profit.

But what if there were a different kind of game—one based on Jesus' view of money? What would it be like?

Form groups of two or three kids each. Distribute copies of "Jesus: The Board Game" (Student Sheet 3), which asks students to create a board game based on the character of Jesus. If needed, refresh their memories about Jesus' attitude toward money by having them read Matthew 5:40-42; 6:19-24.

After several minutes, have each small group explain its version of the "Jesus" game. Then discuss:

What's the objective of your game? (A possibility: To live as simply as you can, and to earn and spend as much as you can to help others.)

What are the starting and finishing points of your game?

What happens along the way?

Do you think most people would want to play your game? Why or why not? (Maybe not, because most people find the idea of amassing wealth for themselves much more appealing than spending it on others.)

Many people aren't interested in Jesus' view of money. In fact, they think what they do with their money is none of God's business. So let's look at the question: "What's God got to do with it?"

This Is My Father's World
Establishing God's Right to Our Finances

Step 2

Pass out hymnals or other copies of the song, "This Is My Father's World." Sing the song or read the lyrics together.

According to this song, who owns the world? (God.)

Why? (Because He made it.)

Now assign individuals to read Psalm 24:1, 2 and Job 41:11.

According to these verses, who owns the world and everything in it? (God.)

Why? (Because He made it.)

Based on these verses, who owns all the wealth in the world? (God.)

Who owns your pet dog, cat, or tropical fish?

Who owns your stereo?

Who owns your family car?

Who owns the money in your pocket or purse?

The answer to these questions is God, but it's an easy answer to give without applying it. Go further with questions like these:

What kind of music should I play if God owns my stereo?

Where should I drive if God owns my car?

Why should I keep anything, or lock the doors to my room or house, if God owns it all?

These are tough questions. Rather than trying to come up with the "right" answers, let kids wrestle with them for a couple of minutes.

How do you feel about the idea of God owning everything—including your money?

Let kids express their feelings before moving to the next activity.

Very Rich and Very Sad
Seeing What God Asked of Some People Who Had Money

Distribute copies of "Thought Balloons" (Student Sheet 4) to the same small groups you used in Step 1. Have students, working in these groups, read the story of the rich young man (Matthew 19:16-26). Kids should then use the passage and their imaginations to come up with the thoughts described in Part I of the sheet. Regather the whole group to discuss answers. Here are some possibilities:

1. The young man as He approached Jesus: "I seem to have everything—but I'm missing one thing. I hope the Teacher can tell me what it is."

2. Jesus, as the man walked away: "He might have made a good disciple—if only his money didn't control him."

3. The man as he walked away: "Why did it have to be money? I would have done anything else for Him."

4. A poor person who saw the whole thing: "Just like the rich. Always following the religious rules, but never willing to part with a penny."

Discuss the passage, using questions like these:

Why was this man sad? (Maybe because He was intrigued by the idea of following Jesus, but realized that the cost—giving up his goods—was too high.)

Didn't the man really want to follow Jesus? (Maybe the man just wanted eternal life and thought he'd get it by doing some small good deed. He seemed to have some desire to do the right thing. But he didn't desire godliness more than he wanted to hold on to his money.)

Does Jesus demand that all people give all their possessions to the poor before they come to Him? If not, why did he demand such a commitment from this man? (Many people don't let their possessions stand in the way of loving God. But people like the young man, who make idols out of their possessions, need to turn from idols and serve the true God [I Thessalonians 1:9].)

Now have the small groups read the story of Ananias and Sapphira (Acts 4:32—5:11), fill out Part II of the student sheet, and share results with the whole group. Here are some thoughts kids might write in the thought balloons:

1. Ananias, approaching the apostles: "We only held back part of the money. The others don't need to know that."

2. Ananias, just before he collapsed: "How did they know? God must see everything after all!"

3. Sapphira, hearing what had happened: "What fools we were—lying to God for the sake of a little money."

4. A wealthy Christian who saw the whole thing: "Wow! I guess I'd better take all this more seriously and not hold back what belongs to God."

What did God want from Ananias and Sapphira? (He wanted them to share their wealth with needy believers, and to be truthful.)

By punishing Ananias and Sapphira, was God forcing the other Chris-

tians to give all their money? (No. Giving the money had been voluntary all along [see 5:4]. The sin of Ananias and Sapphira was lying to God.)

According to Acts 4:32-34, what motivated the Christians to give? (They felt close to each other; they weren't selfish about their possessions and didn't even claim to own them; they wanted to share; they saw that there were needy people among them.)

Which of these words best describes the early Christians' attitude toward honoring God with their money: guilty, fearful, or joyful? (Probably joyful, though some were no doubt fearful about lying after the incident with Ananias and Sapphira.)

Ask kids to think about which of those words—guilty, fearful, or joyful—describes the way they feel about honoring God with their money.

Master Control
Examining Our Attitudes Toward Christ's Lordship

Write the two following sentences on the board:
1. How much of my money should I give to God?
2. How much of God's money should I keep for myself?

According to what we discussed today, which of these questions makes more sense? (The second one, as author Richard Foster has pointed out. God owns everything.)

Pretend for a moment that you own the world and everything in it. You decide to let people use some of your money and possessions. You want these things used in ways that please you. Which of the following systems would you use?
1. **Giving people an allowance—just enough to live on.**
2. **Giving people everything they want.**
3. **Forcing people to use money and things in ways that please you.**
4. **Some other system.**

Let kids respond. If they chose #4, ask them to explain their alternative.

God has chosen an alternative. He shows us He loves us and has our best interests in mind, so that we can choose to love and obey Him. He guides us in the Bible and through His Spirit in the best ways to use money—ways that please Him.

The choice is ours—to serve God or serve money.

Close with silent prayer, asking kids to examine the choices they've been making with money.

When it comes to money and possessions, it seems people never have enough. They want a new album, radio, or car—thinking that when they get it they will be satisfied. But satisfaction seems never to come, and they turn to wanting more new things.

Yet when it comes to God, many people think they have *plenty* of faith and spirituality. God calls us to come closer to Him day by day, but many believers think the faith they had in grade school will get them through life just fine.

That's the paradox. We have an infinite yearning for finite, physical things. But we have a very limited hunger for the deeper spiritual things of life—the only things that make life truly meaningful. This session helps you explore that paradox with your young people.

How Much Is Enough?

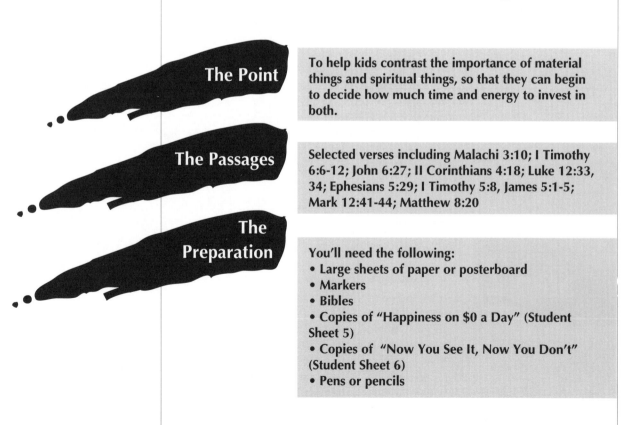

The Point

To help kids contrast the importance of material things and spiritual things, so that they can begin to decide how much time and energy to invest in both.

The Passages

Selected verses including Malachi 3:10; I Timothy 6:6-12; John 6:27; II Corinthians 4:18; Luke 12:33, 34; Ephesians 5:29; I Timothy 5:8, James 5:1-5; Mark 12:41-44; Matthew 8:20

The Preparation

You'll need the following:
• Large sheets of paper or posterboard
• Markers
• Bibles
• Copies of "Happiness on $0 a Day" (Student Sheet 5)
• Copies of "Now You See It, Now You Don't" (Student Sheet 6)
• Pens or pencils

Too Much!
Seeing the Results of Excess as Well as Deprivation

Provide poster-making supplies—markers and large sheets of paper or posterboard—for this activity. Assign each student (or team, if your group is larger), to draw a poster showing what happens when people have too much or too little of one of the following. Each poster should show both the "too much" and "too little" results of the item named.

1. Food
2. Money
3. Work
4. Automobiles
5. Clothing and shoes

When kids have finished their posters, display and discuss them. Here are some results kids might picture:

1. *Too much food:* Overweight, indigestion, etc. *Too little:* Starvation, no resistance to disease.

2. *Too much money:* Worrying about it, defending it, wasting money on luxuries, etc. *Too little:* Poverty, hunger, maybe crime, etc.

3. *Too much work:* Stress, illness, not seeing family, missing other activities, etc. *Too little:* Poverty, boredom, being dependent on others.

4. *Too many automobiles:* Wasting time taking care of them, not using money to help others, having pollution and traffic jams. *Too few:* Not being able to travel or get to the doctor in an emergency.

5. *Too much clothing and shoes:* Spending too much time deciding what to wear, not using money to help others, wasting storage space. *Too little:* Being cold in winter, self-conscious about appearance, etc.

To emphasize the seriousness of excess and deprivation, you may want to mention in the "Too much food" category that one-third of American adults are overweight, some damaging their own health and many limiting their ability to move, play, or work. Under "Too little food," you could mention that 40,000 children die every day around the world from starvation and hunger-related diseases that their weakened bodies are unable to fight.

Can you think of other things people can have too much or too little of? (Recreation, technology, exercise, free time, TV, etc.)

What do you think the following verse means? Read Proverbs 30:7-9. (We should hope for and ask God for just enough—not too little, and not too much. If we have too much, we may take His gifts for granted; too little, and we may feel forced to steal in order to live.)

Needs and Wants
Escaping the Snare of Unlimited Desires

How much is enough? That's a big question. How do you know when you've had enough food? (You feel full—though some people keep right on eating.)

How do you know when you have enough clothes? (Answers will vary: When your closet's full; when you run out of money; when you have the same clothes everybody else does, etc.)

Some people think that as soon as they get those new clothes, or that new car, or that complete album collection, they'll have enough and will be satisfied. But what usually happens? (They still want more.)

Let's see what the Bible says about needs and wants.
Read the following passages and discuss the accompanying questions:
Matthew 8:20

Did Jesus have a home or a job? (Apparently he had no home of his own. He had worked as a carpenter, but apparently not during His three-year ministry.)

Where did He get his food and money? How did he survive? (The Gospels are full of examples of people sharing their homes, meals, and other things with Jesus.)

Does God expect us to live as Jesus did in all ways, including the things found in this verse? (Not necessarily. But when we see how simply Jesus lived, we need to ask ourselves whether we really need most of the things we want.)

I Timothy 6:6-12

What does Paul mean when he tells Timothy about "godliness with contentment"? (Being satisfied in having a relationship with God and with the blessings God has given us.)

Is it really true that we brought nothing into the world and can take nothing out? (We brought—and take—nothing but our souls.)

Is Paul suggesting all Christians should be content with only food and clothing? (These probably stand for all basic needs. Paul wants us to be content with what God has given us and not sin by lusting for more, being tempted by greed, or getting mad at God because we don't have more stuff.)

What are some temptations and traps into which people fall when pursuing riches? (Lying and cheating; stealing; selling drugs; "stepping on" people to get to the top; neglecting their relationship with God and others as they spend all their time making money, etc.)

If all the kids at your school were suddenly content with what they had, what "great gain" might they experience? (Not having to worry about owning the hottest brand of shoes and newest clothes; not having to work a lot of hours after school in order to maintain a car, etc.)

Happiness on $0 a Day
Finding Fun without Spending a Ton

Does being content with what you have mean you have to be miserable for the rest of your life? (Of course not! Otherwise, how could you be content?)

Believe it or not, there are ways to have fun without spending tons of money. But a lot of people don't realize that. Here's an example:

For its 25th Anniversary Tour, the rock band The Who charged $23.50 for tickets. There were additional charges for tax and handling. Parking could cost anywhere from $2 to $5. T-shirts cost $15 or more. Refreshments at the concert could cost anywhere from a few bucks for a drink and chips to more than $10 for hot dogs and nachos. Then there would be the cost of gas to drive to the concert. And there might be a stop at a fast food place before or after the concert. Add it all up and what do you have? Expenses of $25 to $70!

What would be some less expensive ways to hear a concert? (Examples: Watch one on TV or listen to the radio; go to a free or inexpensive concert by a local or even national group.)

Pass out Student Sheet 5, "Happiness on $0 a Day." Working individually or in groups, kids should list some inexpensive alternatives to traditional purchases. Discuss answers afterwards, so each student has even more ideas for spending less money.

Visible and Invisible Wealth

Investing in Things That Last

Think about a person you know who has a lot of money. It can be someone at school or someone you've seen on TV. How do you know this person has a lot of money?

Is this person happy? How do you know?

Point out that it's impossible to really say how happy a person is, based on his or her income. Happiness depends on things we can't see.

There are two worlds: the visible, physical one we live in; and an invisible, spiritual one. God tells us how to have the proper attitude toward both worlds so that our lives are balanced.

Pass out copies of Student Sheet 6, "Now You See It, Now You Don't." Have kids read the instructions, study the verses, and fill in their answers.

Discuss the verses, using questions like these:

In John 6:27, what does "food" stand for? (Things we need. We need some things to survive in this world, but only Christ can give us eternal life.)

How do people "fix their eyes" on earthly or eternal things? (By making these things their goals and spending their lives getting them.)

What do you think people give up to get financial rewards? What do they give up to get eternal rewards?

In Luke 12:33, 34, what are the advantages of "depositing" treasure in heaven? (That treasure won't be exhausted or destroyed. And the process reminds us of what's really important—what's going to last forever.)

What did the rich people in James 5:1-5 do wrong? (They hoarded wealth, indulged themselves, and treated their workers unfairly.)

Ask volunteers to share answers from the second part of Student Sheet 6. Ask why it's hard to be as enthused about eternal rewards as we are about temporary ones. As needed, point out that physical wealth provides immediate gratification. With eternal rewards, satisfaction may come later.

The Mighty Mite

Focusing on How—Not What—We Give

In this session, we've been exploring "How Much Is Enough?" We also need to explore this question: "How much is enough for God?" How much money do you think God wants from each of us?

Let kids discuss their ideas. Then have a student read aloud the story of "The Mighty Mite"—the widow's two coins in Mark 12:41-44. Some versions call her coins "mites," like pennies and nickels in our own day.

Why was the Lord so pleased with such a small offering? (Because it was so much of what the woman had. She had little and gave much.)

Discuss the fact that your kids may not have a lot of money to give. But sometimes God wants us to give Him small, inexpensive things that mean a lot to us. He looks at the heart of the giver—not just at the amount of the gift.

What are some inexpensive—or even free—things you could make available to God for His use? (Examples: A smile, given to that classmate nobody likes; help for someone who has his books knocked out of his hands; help for a slower student who's studying for a test; a sack of fast food for a hungry, homeless person.)

Close by making a list of these suggestions. Encourage kids to choose one to act on during the next 24 hours.

For many North Americans, money is like water: It runs through their fingers. If they fail to be good stewards, it may be partly because they don't see their opportunities for stewardship.

There are many reasons why kids (and adults) tend to spend so much money on themselves and so little on others. They may be unaware of how much money they have—and how little others have. They may be overwhelmed by the problems of world poverty and the need for world evangelism—feeling that any contribution they could make wouldn't have any lasting impact.

But you can help your kids realize their economic power—and their ability to "lay up treasures in heaven." That's the goal of this session.

Where the Smart Money Is

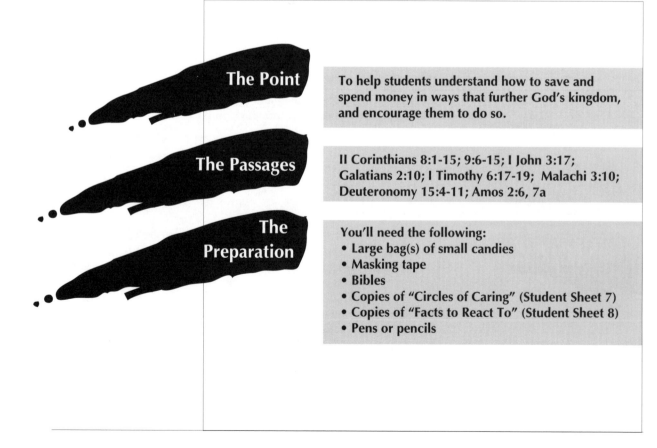

The Point

To help students understand how to save and spend money in ways that further God's kingdom, and encourage them to do so.

The Passages

II Corinthians 8:1-15; 9:6-15; I John 3:17; Galatians 2:10; I Timothy 6:17-19; Malachi 3:10; Deuteronomy 15:4-11; Amos 2:6, 7a

The Preparation

You'll need the following:
• Large bag(s) of small candies
• Masking tape
• Bibles
• Copies of "Circles of Caring" (Student Sheet 7)
• Copies of "Facts to React To" (Student Sheet 8)
• Pens or pencils

Step 1

Your Place in the World
Understanding How Wealthy We Really Are

Most of us think our country is a pretty normal place. The truth of the matter is that it's abnormal, weird, totally unusual!

We're among the world's most well-off citizens. We have only a small percentage of the world's population, but consume a large share of its resources.

To illustrate this, form two groups. Call one "The Developed World," which would include countries like the U.S., Canada, England, Japan, and the Soviet Union. Call the other "The Developing World," which includes "under-developed" places like Haiti, Ethiopia, Bangladesh, parts of Mexico and the Philippines, and other nations.

Using masking tape, make two squares on the floor. Make the "Developed World" square larger than the "Developing World" square. Assign approximately one fourth of your kids to the "Developed World" square, and the remaining three fourths to the "Developing World" square. Kids must stand inside the boundaries of their squares, which should mean crowding for the "Developing World."

Divide one or more large bags of small candies (such as M&M's) between the two groups as follows. First give one candy to each person in the "Developing World" box. Then divide the remainder of the candies among those in the "Developed World" box (providing enough candies so that the latter group gets several per member).

Before long, kids in the "Developing World" box probably will start grumbling. Ask: **What's the matter with you?** (We have more people with fewer resources in less space.)

Ask those in the "Developing World": **How do you feel about the differences between the two groups?**

Discuss the differences, reminding kids that this is a model of the way the real world is.

(Note: This exercise can be adapted for very large groups. Look up country population statistics in a world almanac and divide kids into groups by individual poor and rich countries.)

If you have more than you need and someone else has little or nothing, what are the ways that you could respond? (Ignore the person in need—or share what you have with the person.)

Let's see what the Bible says about our response.

Step 2

Guidebook to Giving
Exploring Biblical Teachings on Sharing Our Wealth

After letting kids leave their squares, arrange them in three study groups. Each should study one of the following passages and summarize for the whole group the principles found in each section.

Group One—II Corinthians 8:1-8

(Theme: Sacrificial giving. Principles: We shouldn't give just when it feels good, but even when it means going without something ourselves. Giving should be something we desire to do, not something we're forced to do. We give ourselves to God first, and to others second.)

Group Two—II Corinthians 8:9-15

(Theme: Christ's example. Principles: Christ was rich, but became poor so that we could be spiritually rich. We should finish what we start, and be consistent in our giving. We should give an appropriate amount, based on what we have been given. Christians should help each other so that all will have enough.)

Group Three—II Corinthians 9:6-15

(Theme: Cheerful giving. Principles: If we scrimp in our giving we will receive little and remain small-hearted. We shouldn't give under pressure, but decide in our own consciences what is an appropriate gift. And when we give, we should do so cheerfully. God will take our gifts and help us grow in our generosity and spiritual maturity. As we give, we will receive what we need in order to give again. We are giving not just to people, but to God Himself, to whom we owe our thanks for everything we have.)

Start with a Tithe
Beginning a Lifestyle of Giving

How do you begin investing in God's work? A good place to start is with tithing.

Read Malachi 3:10. **What were people supposed to do? Why?**

As needed, explain that tithing, which means giving ten percent to God, is a principle that runs throughout the Old Testament. God's people were commanded to give every tenth animal from their flocks and one tenth of their crops as an offering to the Lord.

Help kids figure out what ten percent of their income is. If time allows, hand out scratch paper and ask kids to tally their income from various sources (money from cutting grass or baby-sitting, wages from an after-school job, allowance, etc.) Then ask them to take one-tenth out for God.

If your church takes a position on whether tithing is still mandated today, you could explain that position. In any case, tithing can be a good place to start.

If kids say, "But I can't give; I only get $10 for my allowance," it's a sign that they may not be any more conscientious with $10,000. **If you think you don't have enough money to do anything, do what an author named Richard Foster suggests: Next time you get your paycheck or allowance, get it in $1 bills. Then spread all the bills out on the floor and divide them up for various purposes. It may give you a new way of looking at the dollars you do have to spend!**

Attacking a World of Problems
Overcoming Philanthropic Paralysis

How can you decide where to donate your dollars when so many good organizations promoting so many worthy causes are asking for help?

Distribute Student Sheet 7, "Circles of Caring." Help kids complete Part I, "The Stewardship Bullseye." As you discuss the results, you may want to explain that the model is based on the following two concepts.

1. *Balancing physical and spiritual care.* Some kids will have no problem with this idea. Others, however, may not have heard that caring for people's physical *and* spiritual needs (hunger relief and evangelism, for instance) are both important parts of the Christian life. If so, read passages like these with them: I John 3:17; Galatians 2:10; Deuteronomy 15:4-11; I Timothy 6:17-19.

2. *Setting priorities by geographical distance.* One way to set priorities is to start with local needs (which may have the smallest number of donors to draw on) and work your way "outward." This is one reason why it's so important to financially support your local church.

To help get the ball rolling, here are some possible answers for the innermost circle:

(*Local/Spiritual:* Buying materials for street witnessing in a local park; sponsoring an evangelistic rally or concert; showing a movie with an evangelistic message; helping to buy educational materials for your church, etc. *Local/Physical:* Supporting a local facility for the homeless; providing lunches for elderly people; helping a shelter for battered women, etc.)

After discussing Part I, move on to Part II. Individually or in groups, students should use their answers from Part I to help them decide how to divide the $50 million "pie" left to them by a "rich uncle." Then discuss.

Beyond Band-Aids (optional)
Attacking Root Causes of Poverty

The Old Testament prophets regularly chastised their hearers for sins like sexual transgressions and forgetting to honor and worship God. They also condemned God's people for mistreating the poor.

The Bible indicates that God is deeply concerned about unjust treatment and oppression of the poor. Though this is a complex and controversial subject, this might be the time to get your kids thinking about these big money-related issues.

Read Amos 2:6, 7a. Then pass out copies of "Facts to React To" (Student Sheet 8) and ask kids what they think and feel about the ideas presented there.

Action!
Picking a Project and Getting Started

Whether you want to fight poverty or the systems that cause it, or support local or worldwide evangelism, you can't do much fighting if all you do is talk.

Ask kids to suggest causes, needs, or organizations that could put your group's donations to good use. Bring a few ideas of your own, too. Decide with the group which cause to support. Then decide how you will collect money, how much you need, who will supervise sending it off or delivering it, and how the entire group can hear about the results of the giving.

Note: If you want to help kids further explore how they can make a difference, here are two Christian organizations that offer free materials designed for youth groups.

1. Mission Aviation Fellowship offers the "Air Care" package, complete with a video and other resources. Call (714) 794-1151.

2. Compassion International offers the Compassion Project, a curriculum resource containing two videos, a leader's notebook, slides, posters, music tapes, and a book of service projects. Call 1-800-336-7676.

You may also want to check on resources available from your church or denomination, or from missionaries who live in your area.

Remember Nehru jackets? Bell-bottom jeans? Hula hoops? Pet rocks?

History is full of fads and fashions that have come and gone with lightning speed. Such fads are just one way enterprenuers have to separate you from your money. Another is "planned obsolescence," which means that even if your 1962 Rambler is running just fine, the new models out of Detroit and Tokyo will embarrass you into buying a new car anyway.

This session takes a look at how young spenders can avoid some of the traps that waste money. It also helps you suggest ways in which they can save and invest money in order to further the kingdom of God.

Don't Let It Slip Away

The Point — To help kids conserve and increase resources for God's work by wise spending and investing.

The Passages — Matthew 25:14-30; Proverbs 6:6-11; 21:20; 31:10-31; Ecclesiates 7:12; Luke 8:1-3; John 19:38-40

The Preparation — You'll need the following:
• Several $5 or $10 bills
• Two envelopes, matches, and a metal pie plate
• Bibles
• Copies of "Bargain Hunter's Toolbox" (Student Sheet 9)
• Newspapers, posterboard, scissors, fad items (optional)
• Chalkboard and chalk or newsprint and marker

Money to Burn
Seeing the Need to Watch Where Our Money Goes

Before the session, hide a sealed envelope in your pocket.

When the session starts, hold up several $5 or $10 bills. **See this money?** Let a group member count it. Seal the bills in a second envelope and put it in your pocket with the empty envelope. **Let's come up with a list of all the good things we could do with this money—including things that help other people.**

Spend a couple of minutes brainstorming. List kids' ideas on the board or newsprint. Then pull out the empty envelope, pretending it's the "real" one. Place it on a metal pie plate.

Let's vote. Which of the good causes on the list should I use this money for? Have the group vote.

Well, thanks for the suggestion. But I think I'll do something else with this money. Strike a match and set the envelope on fire—which will probably cause some consternation in the group.

What's wrong? Don't you think that was a good use of the money? Let kids respond. Explain that most of us "burn" money every week—by letting it slip through our fingers. In this session you'll discuss how to make the most of money instead of wasting it. (You might also show kids the bills in your pocket to assure them that you didn't really burn them.)

Buried Treasure
Seeing that God Cares How We Use Money

God holds us accountable for the things He's entrusted to us. That principle applies to money—as well as to the rest of life.

Have volunteers take turns reading the parable of the talents (Matthew 25:14-30) aloud. Explain that a talent was a type of money worth more than $1,000.

Discuss the parable, using questions like these:

What did the master want the servants to do with the money? (Invest it; make it grow.)

Who would benefit from wise use of the money? (The master would benefit by increasing his wealth; the servants would benefit by earning more responsibility.) Observe that the point was to please the master, not just to make the money grow.

What are some ways to "bury" your money? (Wasting it, spending it all on yourself instead of "investing" in eternal treasures, not saving any of it, not doing anything with it that pleases God, etc.)

What's one way to invest your money that you think would please God?

Investors and Savers
Discovering Biblical Advice on Handling Resources Wisely

Form three groups. Have each group look up its verses as follows; group members should be ready to tell what the verses say about using finances wisely. Use the discussion questions as needed.

Group One—Proverbs 6:6-11; 21:20; Ecclesiastes 7:12

(Like an ant stores provisions, we should save money for future needs;

don't spend all your money; money can shelter or protect us, though it can't protect us from everything.)

What do you find hardest about saving money?

What's something you've "saved up for"?

How could you use money to shelter or protect another person?

Group Two—Proverbs 31:10-31

(The virtuous woman works willingly and earns money; she plans ahead; she thinks before buying and makes wise purchases; she makes a profit and invests it; she shares her resources with the needy; she has a business of her own; she keeps track of her money.)

How much thought do you put into your purchases?

When you make some money, what do you usually do with it?

Group Three—Luke 8:1-3; John 19:38-40

(Women used their money to support Jesus and His disciples; Nicodemus and Joseph of Arimathea used their money to honor Jesus by providing for His burial.)

A lot of people today are working to honor Jesus by telling others about Him. If you had to choose one such worker to support with your money, who would it be? If kids have trouble coming up with names, this would be a good time to mention the missionaries your church supports.

Step 4

Bargain Hunter's Toolbox
Learning How to Save a Bundle

Everybody has to buy things. But not everybody buys things wisely. Looking for bargains is biblical, and it makes a lot of sense. If you save money on a purchase, you have more money left—either for yourself or to support other causes.

Distribute copies of "Bargain Hunter's Toolbox" (Student Sheet 9). Read and discuss the money-saving suggestions there. If you have time, use some of the following activities to help kids practice and remember the suggestions on the sheet:

1. Use Sunday advertisements.

Before the session, go through some of these ads and cut out items you think your kids may have purchased or may soon purchase—sports accessories, clothing, music, electronic appliances, etc. Paste the photos of these items to a piece of posterboard, hiding the prices. Discuss non-sale prices some of your students may have paid.

2. Check classified ads.

Bring in a newspaper classified section and show kids how to use it.

3. Watch display ads.

Pass out a newspaper or two and have kids do some comparison shopping for a common grocery item.

4. Phone first.

Before the session, call three stores and ask their prices for a cassette player. Make sure you get prices for the same brand and model. Present the price differences to your group. Or assign a couple of kids to do some comparison shopping over the phone during the coming week, checking on items like one gallon of regular unleaded gasoline or the cost of a hamburger, medium soft drink, and fries.

5. Clip coupons.

Have teams clip coupons from identical newspapers, seeing who can come up with the greatest total savings in two minutes.

6. Buy used stuff instead of new.

Discuss what kids (or their parents) have found at garage sales and secondhand stores.

7. Stay away from fads.

If possible, show some relics of old fads from your own closet. Tell how these items came into your possession. Discuss the fads of yesteryear and what they meant to you and your friends.

What are today's hot fads, and what are kids buying to keep in step?

Are there faddish purchases you've made in the past and now regret?

Well Done?

Evaluating Our Financial Habits

Ask kids to bow their heads and think about the parable of the talents again. Ask them to think about this question, too:

If God had a talk with you about the way you've been using money, do you think He'd say, "Well done, good and faithful servant"? Why or why not?

Close in prayer.

Win, Lose, or Draw

For each person described, write "W" if you think the person is a winner; "L" if you think he or she is a loser; or "D" if you don't know.

___ Person A has a car that barely runs and has rust holes all over it.

___ Person B makes $20,000 a year driving a bus.

___ Person C makes $150,000 a year selling illegal drugs.

___ Person D has five children.

___ Person E is 32 years old and not married.

___ Person F has a new Lamborghini sports car, a motorcycle, and a small private plane.

___ Person G works in the warehouse at a lumber yard.

___ Person H is a college professor.

___ Person I is on welfare.

___ Person J won $2 million in the lottery.

___ Person K can't afford to go to college.

___ Person L reads the Bible every day.

___ Person M has a whole room for playing video games.

___ Person N is confined to a wheel-chair.

___ Person O has been on the honor roll for two years.

More Than Money

What do you want to do when you "grow up"? How do you decide?

Here's a list of jobs. Down the right side of the sheet are four columns listing factors to be considered when looking at jobs and careers.

Fill out the chart by giving each job a rating of 1 to 10 (10 being highest or best) in each of the four categories. Then write in two other jobs or careers you might be interested in—and rate them, too.

	Earnings (1-10)	Personal Satisfaction (1-10)	Service to People (1-10)	Service to God (1-10)
Sunday School Teacher or Youth Worker				
Architect				
Nurse				
Personnel Manager				
Auto Mechanic				
School Teacher				
Movie Star				
Other (Name):				
Other (Name):				

Jesus: The Board Game

Multimillionaire Donald Trump had a board game named after him and based on his approach to money. Why isn't there a board game based on the approach of Jesus? You can help create such a game by filling out this sheet.

Objective of "Trump":
Get rich. Invest in properties. Sell at a higher price. Be a winner at the entrepreneurial game.

Objective of "Monopoly":
Own—or control—all the properties on the board. Charge your opponent rent until he or she goes bankrupt.

Objective of "Jesus: The Board Game":

Would you use money in the "Jesus" game? How?

Let your imagination go wild! Draw a game board that shows how your version of **"Jesus: The Board Game"** might work.

Thought Balloons

Part I

Read the story of the rich young man (Matthew 19:16-26). In the "thought balloons," write what each of the people involved might have been thinking.

1. The young man as He approached Jesus 2. Jesus, as the man walked away 3. The man as he walked away 4. A poor person who saw the whole thing

Part II

Now read the story of Ananias and Sapphira (Acts 5:1-11). In the thought balloons, write what each of these people involved might have been thinking.

1. Ananias, approaching the apostles 2. Ananias, just before he collapsed 3. Sapphira, hearing what had happened 4. A wealthy Christian who saw the whole thing

Happiness on $0 a Day

Ever seen those books with titles like *Europe on $5 a Day* or *Antarctica on 25 Cents a Week*? There's another fun place where we can all spend a lot less money than many people do: Right where we are!

Here's a list of activities. For each one, list how much money it might cost; one or more free or cheap alternatives; and possible advantages to the alternatives. An example is provided.

After you've filled out the sheet, think about ways you can have more fun while spending less money.

Activity	Cost	Alternative	Advantage
Concert	$25-$70	Local concert in park	Cheaper; probably nobody will throw up on you or break off your car's radio antenna. Plus you get to see squirrels while the music is playing.
Going to a movie			
Dining out			
Buying birthday presents			
Buying a new tape or compact disc			
Other (name)			

Now You See It, Now You Don't

There are two kinds of wealth: visible (the kind that "pays off" now) and invisible (the kind that "pays off" in heaven). Read these passages which discuss the two kinds of wealth:

John 6:27
II Corinthians 4:18
Luke 12:33, 34
James 5:1-5

After thinking about visible and invisible wealth, take a look at the actions below. Can you think of visible rewards you might get from some of them? How about invisible, eternal rewards? Some may have both. Be ready to explain your answers, and to think about how much time, money and energy you're willing to devote to these two different kinds of wealth.

Action	Visible Rewards?	Eternal Rewards?
Working part-time after school		
Giving money to a missionary		
Buying your girl-friend/boyfriend a gift		
Giving a dollar to a homeless person		
Giving a coat to a homeless person		
Putting a little spare change in the offering plate		
Buying the video of your favorite movie		
Renting a children's video and watching it with your little brother or sister		
Saving your money for a youth group retreat		
Buying your lunch in the school cafeteria		

Circles of Caring

Part I: The Stewardship Bullseye

The world has so many needs! How can one person decide which ones to try to meet?

The Stewardship Bullseye is designed to help. It divides the world into four areas. The rings represent four increasingly large areas: your local area or city; your state or province; your country; and the world.

The bullseye is also divided into two types of needs—spiritual and physical.

Try to identify one important need for each of the eight sections of the bullseye. Write your answers in the sections.

Spiritual   Worldwide / National / Regional / Local   **Physical**

Part II: Dividing the Pie

Imagine that an incredibly rich uncle has just died. You've been left in charge of his $100 million estate. You'll get $50 million yourself when you reach the age of 21. But in the meantime, it's your responsibility to divide up the other $50 million among organizations and causes which, in the words of your uncle's will, "benefit God and people."

Using the social or spiritual needs you listed on the Stewardship Bullseye, divide up the $50 million as you'd want to donate it. Remember that the whole pie chart represents the whole $50 million.

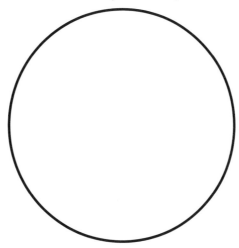

Facts to React To

Here, from Ron Sider's book, *Rich Christians in an Age of Hunger* (InterVarsity Press), are a few facts to consider:

- The world's developed countries have only 25 percent of the world's population, but consume between 83 percent and 94 percent of its resources.
- Two-thirds of the world's annual catch of tuna goes to the United States, and a third of that is used to make cat food.
- The United States uses 5.2 million tons of grain each year in the production of alcoholic beverages. That much grain could feed 26 million hungry people in one of the world's underdeveloped countries.

See whether you agree with the following suggestions from Ron Sider. Be ready to explain your answers.

- We need "to move toward a personal lifestyle that could be sustained for a long period of time if it were shared by everyone in the world."
- "We need to distinguish between necessities and luxuries."
- "Expenditures for the purpose of status, pride, staying in fashion, and 'keeping up with the Joneses' are wrong."

Bargain Hunter's Toolbox

Everybody has to buy things. But not everybody buys things wisely. Looking for bargains is not only biblical, it makes a lot of sense. If you save money on a purchase, you have more money left—either for yourself or to support other causes.

Here are just a few ways to be a wiser buyer:

1. *Use Sunday advertisements.*

Every Sunday, newspapers across the country are full of full-color ads for practically everything in the universe. Look for sales on things you already plan to buy.

2. *Check classified ads.*

Most newspaper classified ad sections have a "merchandise mart" department where people offer everything from sofas to stereos.

3. *Watch display ads.*

During the week, many stores advertise sales on the pages of the newspaper.

4. *Phone first.*

Sit down and let your fingers do the walking. Call at least three stores, if possible, and ask their prices for the item you want.

5. *Clip coupons.*

Coupons are everywhere: in the newspaper, in magazines, in your mailbox, and plastered all over bulletin boards in supermarkets. Also, some fast food restaurants give away discount coupons for promotional purposes.

6. *Buy used stuff instead of new.*

Does everything you buy have to be new? Check garage sales, flea markets, discount shops, used record and book outlets, and other stores. You may find real bargains there.

7. *Stay away from fads.*

Remember the hula hoop, the Nehru jacket, love beads, bell-bottom pants, and disco shirts? Probably not. They were fads of the fifties, sixties, and seventies.

Fads are fun, but they're also very expensive. When mood rings or Batman decals are hot, they're hot. But when fads cool down, these trinkets wind up in the bottom of a desk drawer or closet before they make their final journey to the junk heap.

Buy smart! Make your next purchases investments in quality and efficiency—not rash expenditures for cheap, passing fads.

How to Talk to Kids about Creation and Evolution

by Dr. Larry Richards

"Wait a minute! Me? Me lead a unit on creation and evolution? Hey, I'm no expert!"

If that's your reaction to the discovery that creation and evolution are next up on your group's menu, I've got good news. You don't have to be an expert. Your kids don't expect you to be an expert. And it doesn't take an expert to be of real help to young people, who do have questions about what they probably think is a conflict between the Bible and science.

Here are some hints for "non-experts"—hints that will make your job of leading these sessions a little easier.

Starting Off

When the teens at our church wanted to look at this issue, the leaders first took a poll. That poll showed that our teens were evenly divided: Half tended to accept what they'd been taught in school; the other half thought the Bible contradicted evolutionary theory and chose to believe the Bible.

This may be a good way to prepare your own kids for this unit on creation and evolution. Try taking a poll. Compile the results and give your group feedback on what members think (without naming names). Use these questions as starters, and add a few of your own:

• Which do you think is more likely— creation or evolution?

• Do most people you know believe in creation or in evolution?

• Do you ever wonder if there is good, scientific support for the Bible's teaching on creation?

• Do you think there is good, scientific evidence for evolution?

• Do you think a Christian can believe in both the Bible and evolution? Why or why not?

• Do you think it makes any real difference whether God created the universe or it just evolved?

Kids seldom talk with each other about creation and evolution. But they do think about it. Many Christian teens feel uncertain about the subject, especially those who attend schools where biblical creationism is dismissed as foolishness and evolution is presented as scientific fact. So it's not surprising that Christian teens have questions. They wonder what others think. They wonder what the Bible really does teach. And they wonder if creationism is intellectually defensible.

By taking that initial poll, you let your kids know that this time they'll be able to raise their questions and even express their doubts.

What You Won't Need to Know

I really meant it when I said you won't need to be an expert to lead these sessions. Here are some of the things you *won't* need to know to do a great job:

• You won't need to know answers to tough scientific questions. Very few teens have the background to get into complicated technical questions. So don't worry if you aren't sure why left-handed amino acids are important evidence against the chance evolution of living creatures.

• You won't need to memorize the geologic table or explain where dinosaurs fit into the Book of Genesis. You'll have enough background in the session plans to orient you to things most teens want to know and probably will ask about.

• You won't have to answer difficult theology questions. Instead, you'll look with your teens into key Bible passages that present Scripture's view of creation.

But what if you do get a tough question you can't answer? One way to handle that is to have the person who raised the question, or a volunteer, study up on the subject and give a report the following week. Another is to have a good resource book handy, ready to refer to. I'd suggest *It Couldn't Just Happen* (Word, 1988), a book I wrote for teens. *It Couldn't Just Happen* surveys relevant fields of science and shows that the weight of scientific evidence is actually on the side of creationism.

So don't worry about not having all the answers. Between guidance you receive in these session plans, plus resource books that are available, you'll have plenty of help.

What You Will Need to Know

Some terms used in talking about creation and evolution are confusing. You will want to know what several terms mean, and keep those meanings clear during this study. Here are definitions you'll surely want to know.

Two meanings of the word "evolution." Most people probably think of evolution as a sweeping theory—the idea that everything took gradual form over billions of years, and all living things, including man, developed gradually from single-celled animals that themselves came into existence by random combination of non-living matter.

The Bible, which teaches that God personally created the universe, living things, and by a special act created human beings, is in direct conflict with this kind of evolution.

But there is another kind of evolution. It describes the changes we observe taking place in nature today through processes such as natural selection. The Bible has no conflict with this kind of evolution. It's important when you and your teens are talking about this topic not to confuse the two kinds of evolution.

Scientific fact. The scientific method is the approach scientists use to gather information from the world of nature. A scientific fact is information that has been validated by repeated observation and experimentation. Scientists use the information they gather to develop theories, which they then test by further observation and experimentation.

The evolutionary theory about how the universe and life began is not a "scientific fact." At best scientists can only reason from information we have about the world of nature, and then guess what might have happened in the beginning to make the world what it is today.

Creationism is the theory that God brought the universe into existence and gave life to all living creatures. In other words, what exists today didn't "just happen," but is a result of the purposeful action of a personal God. While Christians may accept creationism on the basis of the Bible, it's important to know that many believing scientists are convinced that "scientific facts" actually give more support to the theory of creation than to the theory of evolution.

If you can keep the real meaning of these terms clear during this unit, it will help your teens realize that the creation/evolution debate isn't a debate between the Bible and science at all. It's a difference of opinion as to whether what we have learned about our universe supports the biblical view of origins, or the view expressed in the theory of evolution.

What's Your Goal?

In this unit you have an important but limited goal: To help your teens grow in their confidence that the biblical account is accurate, and that God is the Creator.

During these sessions your teens will find out that Christians who believe in creation have different ways of interpreting the Bible's account. Some think Creation took place in seven consecutive 24-hour days; others think that a gap of millions of years may follow each day of Genesis 1. Some argue that Creation took place as little as 15,000 years ago; others think it took place millions or even billions of years in the past.

It's important as you discuss questions like these not to be dogmatic. Why? Because there's no way to tell who's right! The Bible doesn't say, for example, that Creation took place at 9 A.M. on June 24th, 15,086 B.C. Since Scripture doesn't speak out on this or similar issues, it's wisest if we admit that we don't know just when God created, or even exactly how. In fact, the Hebrew word for "create" *(bara')* does *not* mean to "make something out of nothing," as is commonly thought. The Hebrew word means "to initiate an object or project." The issue of creation from nothing must be settled on other grounds.

And it's this that you want your teens to gain from their study: A fresh confidence that, even though we can't say just when or how, God in fact did set our universe in motion. Everything that is, including every human being, goes back to the very beginning where we find God.

Larry Richards is author of over 100 books, including It Couldn't Just Happen, *which received the Evangelical Christian Publishers' Association Gold Medallion award as the best Christian Education book published in 1988. He is also the author of* Teens: Giving Youth the Grow-Ahead *(David C. Cook). Dr. Richards' textbooks are used in many Christian colleges and seminaries, and have been translated into 17 foreign languages.*

CREATION AND EVOLUTION

by Dave and Neta Jackson

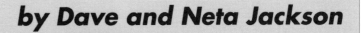

Dave and Neta Jackson are free-lance writers and editors in Evanston, Illinois. Dave is a former pastor. He and Neta have written more than 20 books—and have co-written many more, including *Teen Pregnancy* (David C. Cook).

Have you ever seen the film *Inherit the Wind,* the dramatic portrayal of the famous 1925 Scopes "monkey trial" in Tennessee? If so, your emotions may have bounced between enthusiasm and embarrassment as William Jennings Bryan (played by Fredric March) and Clarence Darrow (played by Spencer Tracy) debated the merits of creation and evolution.

Darrow's efforts to defend John T. Scopes' right to teach evolution in Tennessee's public schools appear strangely ironic alongside the efforts of some Christians to secure the right to present the creation "alternative" in today's public schools.

Some adults think the controversy between creation and evolution shouldn't make any difference to one's basic faith. But that's not the way many kids experience it. Kids find it profoundly disturbing that science describes the universe and its origins in ways that seem to contradict what the Bible says. And in this technology-oriented era, their faith is what gives ground too often.

You'll want to stay close to your kids as you lead them through one or more of these sessions, exploring the work of God the Creator and ways to understand how He did it all.

What's the Difference?

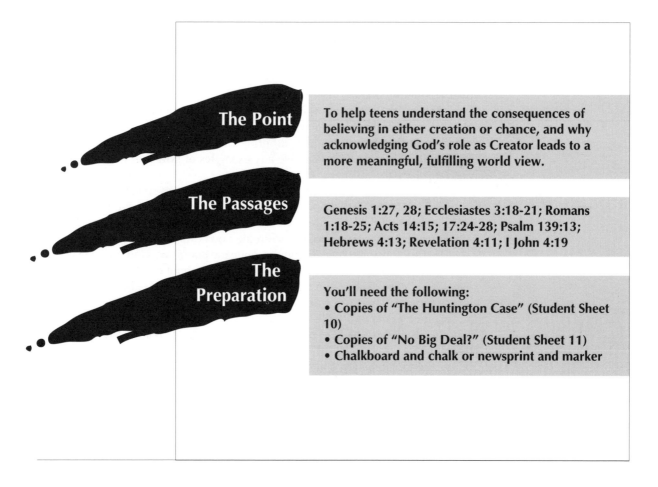

The Point

To help teens understand the consequences of believing in either creation or chance, and why acknowledging God's role as Creator leads to a more meaningful, fulfilling world view.

The Passages

Genesis 1:27, 28; Ecclesiastes 3:18-21; Romans 1:18-25; Acts 14:15; 17:24-28; Psalm 139:13; Hebrews 4:13; Revelation 4:11; I John 4:19

The Preparation

You'll need the following:
• Copies of "The Huntington Case" (Student Sheet 10)
• Copies of "No Big Deal?" (Student Sheet 11)
• Chalkboard and chalk or newsprint and marker

The Great Whodunit
Seeing the Implications of Different Views

Before class, cut apart the character descriptions from "The Huntington Case" (Student Sheet 10). Give roles to four students without letting any one of them know what descriptions the other students receive.

Explain to the rest of the group that each person in the room is a detective on Scotland Yard's new investigative team. The team has been called to a large Gothic mansion in the English countryside, where the body of young M.R. Huntington, Esquire, has been discovered crumpled by the fireplace in the large ballroom.

There are four people to question:

1. Mrs. Huntington, the deceased's elderly mother.

2. Constable McDoogle, the first police officer on the scene.

3. Farley, the faithful butler for 33 years who will inherit the whole estate when Mrs. Huntington dies.

4. Mildred Walters, the beautiful maid. Everyone knows she's had an unreturned crush on M.R. since they were children.

Instruct the class to question the four about M. R.'s untimely death. Each role-player's answers should be consistent with his or her description on the sheet.

After questioning has gone on for a few minutes, interrupt the process and ask: **How might the viewpoint of each character confuse the investigation?**

List responses on the chalkboard or newsprint. They might include some of the following:

• If it was murder, Mrs. Huntington's efforts to focus only on her grief might allow a murderer to go free, possibly endangering herself.

• Even though Farley didn't commit murder, his selfish desire to inherit the estate led him to lie by writing a false suicide note—which could backfire and make him appear guilty.

• The constable's drive to arrest someone quickly might lead to his overlooking the truth.

Solving the case isn't our purpose today. The point is to see how the characters' differing viewpoints lead to confusion. It's the same way with creation and evolution. People's differing viewpoints affect the way they investigate this issue. Can you give any examples of how that might work? As needed, share the following examples:

1. Just as the truth mattered for Mrs. Huntington, even though she denied it, so it matters in the question of creation and evolution. Some Christians want to ignore the whole question. They don't realize that in the long run it may affect people's faith—maybe even their own.

2. Farley wanted to score big, so he made claims beyond what he knew to be true. Some Christians claim to know "facts" about creation and evolution even though the details aren't conclusive. Their motives may be good, but the whole thing can backfire when later information is uncovered.

3. Just as the constable's rush to make an arrest might have led to a serious mistake, hurrying to pin down all the details of creation may hurt more than it helps.

Exploring creation and evolution is something like a whodunit. Did life evolve on its own out of energy and matter that has always existed? Or did God, as Creator, design and bring the universe into existence? Did He create life? Did He create human beings, or did they evolve on their own from lower forms of life?

Ask kids whether they've seen or read *Inherit the Wind*, the drama about the famous 1925 Scopes "monkey trial." If kids have seen or read the play, ask how they felt as the main characters debated the merits of creation and evolution. If they haven't seen it, ask how they feel when the origins of life are discussed in school or on TV.

As in the Huntington Case, how we approach a mystery may influence our conclusions. So it's important to see what the main claim of the Bible is on the question of how life came to be.

The Bottom Line
Discovering the Main Biblical Claim about Origins

Have volunteers look up, read, and summarize the following passages. List results on the board or newsprint. Summaries might look like these:

Acts 14:15—God made everything.
Acts 17:24-28—God made all people and cares about them.
John 1:3, 4—God is the source of life.
Genesis 1:27, 28—God created the human race in His image.
Psalm 139:13—God is active in our personal formation.
Hebrews 4:13—We are accountable to God, who sees all.
Revelation 4:11—God, the Creator, is worthy of worship.

What's the bottom line of these verses? If you combine what they say, what's the big, main message? (That God is Creator.) Explain that during your discussions of creation and evolution, you'll keep coming back to this foundational fact: God is the Creator.

The Bible clearly declares God to be the Creator. It's also honest enough to report that not everyone believes this message. Ask a student to read Psalm 14:1. **Have you heard anyone say there is no God? What reasons did he or she give?**

Read Romans 1:18-25. **How are God's power and nature evident to all people?** (In creation.)

What happened when people rejected the evidence about God? (Their minds and hearts were darkened; they became fools; they worshiped idols; God let them degrade themselves with their sin.)

What "idols" do some people choose to trust in today instead of trusting God? (Money, fame, achievements, weapons, etc.)

What's at Stake?
Seeing the Interdependency of the Scriptures

The Bible has a lot to say about history, among other things. One aspect of history that the Bible addresses is the origin and design of the universe. This is where the creation/evolution controversy comes up.

What would it do to your faith if you discovered that the Bible was not accurate on some historical points?

What would it do to your faith if you discovered that God had no hand in Creation, that all things evolved from matter and energy that have always existed?

Kids may admit that their faith would be shaken. Point out that the Scriptures are an interdependent whole; rejecting the reliability of any part ultimately weakens the rest.

One student said after taking a course in evolution that she could keep

believing in God only by "compartmentalizing" Him and His acts. She decided to make God and the Bible apply only to her "spiritual" life. But she confessed that even that approach isn't so easy. She said, "I suppose if you took evolution to its inevitable conclusion, you have atheism." Do you agree?

Truth or Consequences
Understanding the Character of a World without God

When people ignore or deny their Creator, what happens? Look again at Romans 1:18-25. (Society goes wild as God lets people indulge sinful desires.)

Distribute copies of Student Sheet 11, "No Big Deal?" Have volunteers read aloud items from the sheet.

Do any of these sound like the people described in the Romans passage? (Yes.) Why? (Some of them put their own interests first, take serious things lightly, don't care about God's standards of right and wrong, etc.)

Look again at the summaries from Step 2. Which of the principles we found in these passages are being ignored by the people in the news items? (The idea that God cares about all people; that each person is valuable because God made humans in His image and continues to watch over each person's development; that we are accountable to God, who sees all.)

When people believe they're the product of a process that doesn't require a Creator, they don't have much reason to feel accountable to anyone or anything outside themselves. They soon make their own interests their gods. When that happens, who decides what is right and wrong? (God's standards continue to exist, but whatever group of people is strongest usually imposes its will on the rest.)

Would you want to live in a world where no one believed God created the universe? Why or why not?

Who Cares?
Seeing How Our View of Creation Really Matters

How could exploring the issue of creation and evolution be important to the following people?

1. A student in biology class. (May want to respond to what the teacher or textbook says about evolution; may be confused about what to believe.)

2. A girl who feels worthless, that no one cares about her. (Needs to know she has been created by the God who loves her.)

3. A guy who believes in creation just because his parents do. (Should prepare for challenges he'll face from skeptics; may not grow in his faith unless he thinks the issue through for himself.)

4. A student who is interested in Jesus, but has heard Christians are ignorant and backward about science. (Needs to know whether a belief in creation makes sense.)

5. A person who is ready to throw away biblical standards of behavior because "the Bible's full of mistakes anyway." (Needs to know whether the Bible's account of creation can be trusted.)

6. You. Let kids reply or just think about this.

If you plan to use other sessions in this unit, tell kids that you'll be exploring creation and evolution in detail during the weeks to come. You may want to invite them to submit questions to you for future discussion.

"Three and a half million years ago, in East Africa, man stood up and began to prowl the earth."
—from the historical introduction to *Bagamoyo*, a novel by Betty and Jock Leslie-Melville

In the arts, the physical sciences, the social sciences, the news media, and school textbooks, evolution is almost everywhere accepted as an incontestable fact. But your kids need to know that some scientists, theologians, and other experts see things differently—and why.

This session begins to explore the reasons for apparent conflicts between current scientific knowledge and the Genesis account of creation. Instead of offering simple answers, it helps young people wrestle with the most important questions.

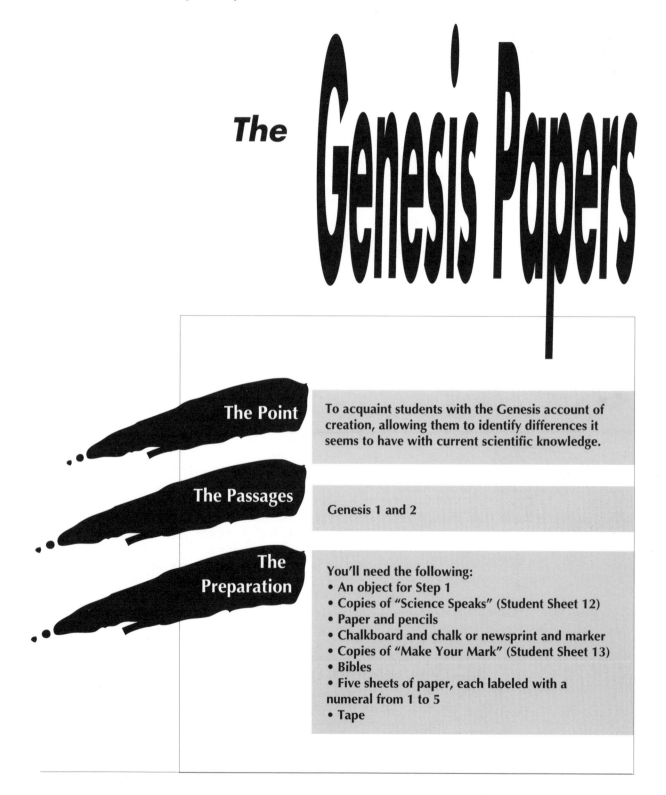

The Genesis Papers

The Point — To acquaint students with the Genesis account of creation, allowing them to identify differences it seems to have with current scientific knowledge.

The Passages — Genesis 1 and 2

The Preparation — You'll need the following:
- An object for Step 1
- Copies of "Science Speaks" (Student Sheet 12)
- Paper and pencils
- Chalkboard and chalk or newsprint and marker
- Copies of "Make Your Mark" (Student Sheet 13)
- Bibles
- Five sheets of paper, each labeled with a numeral from 1 to 5
- Tape

Where Did It Come From?

Thinking about Different Ways to See Origins

Bring a household item to class. It could be practically anything—a flashlight, a pillow, a frozen TV dinner, etc. Place the object where the whole group can see it.

Where did this thing come from? How did it come to exist? That's the question we have to answer.

Form four teams. The first team should try to come up with a technical answer—explaining how the item was manufactured. The second team should concentrate on how the inventor might have conceived and perfected the item. The third team should concentrate on God's role (creating raw materials, giving people the ability to invent and manufacture, etc.). The fourth team should come up with a wild and crazy explanation.

After a few minutes, regather the whole group and have teams share their explanations. Then ask:

Why are these explanations different? (They started with different purposes.)

Which explanation is best? (It depends on what you want to know about the item's origin. If you want to be entertained instead of informed, the wild and crazy explanation might be best.)

Where you end up often depends on where you start. How you explain the origins of life and the universe depends on your assumptions, too. We're going to begin exploring the creation/evolution controversy by looking at two starting points—in science and in the Bible.

Where Do We Start?

Identifying Bases of Various Theories of Origins

Distribute copies of "Science Speaks" (Student Sheet 12). Cover the content of the sheet by either (1) having kids take turns reading it aloud, (2) paraphasing it yourself, or (3) having one advanced student play the role of a scientist and read it.

Then discuss the main points from the sheet. The following may help:

Think back to our explanations of where that object (in Step 1) came from. What would most scientists think of them? (Scientists would like the technical explanation if it were based on observation. They might consider the theory about the inventor if it could be based reasonably on observation. They probably would not consider the explanation involving God's role, since it could not be proven strictly by observation. And they would discard the wild and crazy explanation as involving "unnatural" laws.)

Could you prove, using only the scientific method of observation and testing, that God created the universe and gave life to all living things? (Not really.) Explain that this biblical claim can't be proven true or false at this time by scientific inquiry. But that doesn't make it an invalid claim. It simply makes it a theological claim. There is biblical proof and substantial scientific *support*—but not scientific *proof.*

What Does It Say?

Discovering What Genesis 1 Says

When it comes to our beginnings, the bottom line in the Bible is that God created the universe and gave life to every living thing. That theme appears in many passages.

But the first chapters of Genesis seem to detail how, in what order, and (by implication) when God created things. That's where evolutionary theories and the Bible seem to be most at odds.

Assign small groups or individuals to look up the following accounts of each day of creation in Genesis 1. Each person or small group should be ready to tell in simple, straightforward terms what the Bible says happened on that day.

Day One—Genesis 1:3-5
Day Two—Genesis 1:6-8
Day Three—Genesis 1:9-13
Day Four—Genesis 1:14-19
Day Five—Genesis 1:20-23
Day Six—Genesis 1:24-27, 31

Before kids report their findings, read Genesis 1:1, 2 to set the stage for the creation story. Then, as the kids report, list their findings on the chalkboard or newsprint. Conclude that part of the discussion by reading the summary of creation in Genesis 2:1.

Do you see any problems in the first chapter of Genesis? These could include statements that seem to disagree with each other, statements that don't agree with what we see in the world around us, and statements that seem to conflict with what science tells us.

Students may point out the following:

• Light existed (vs. 3) before its sources were created (vs. 14).

• Light was separated from darkness (vs. 4) before God created the means of separating light from darkness (vs. 14).

• It appears that much of the earth's water was positioned above the earth, separated from earth (and the rest of the water on the earth) by "sky."

• If the six days of creation are consecutive 24-hour days, that seems in conflict with the billions of years that the geologic record seems to suggest elapsed during creation.

• Birds appeared before land animals.

Point out, however, that apart from these seeming conflicts, most of the creation account in Genesis 1 follows a sequence of events quite similar to that described by science:

1. A barren earth racked by geologic upheaval is finally stabilized (vs. 9).
2. Plant life appears (vs. 11).
3. Sea creatures appear (vss. 20, 21).
4. Land animals appear (vs. 24).
5. Humans appear last as the highest form of life (vs. 27).

Now ask a volunteer to read Genesis 2:2-4. Point out that this is the conclusion of the first chapter's creation account. Then ask another volunteer to read Genesis 2:5-7, 19 (or 5-25 if you have time). This, too, is a creation account.

What differences do you see between the two accounts? (The second one doesn't limit creation to individual acts on consecutive days; both man and animals are said to be made out of "the ground," a detail not mentioned in the first chapter.)

Why Does It Say That?
Discovering the Genesis Perspective

How do you feel when you see apparent conflicts, even little ones, in what the Bible says about creation? (Probably worried, bothered, confused, etc.)

Explain that Christians have interpreted the Genesis account in different ways, and knowing those can help us deal with the contradictions. If you plan to use Session 4 in this unit, you'll address interpretations then. For now, point out the need to understand how God's Word approaches the whole job of describing creation. For one thing, the Bible doesn't try to establish its facts through a scientific argument.

Read or paraphrase the following quote from a professor of physics and astronomy:

"The Bible does not describe the Creation in the language of modern natural science. But neither does the Bible speak in the language of ancient science. . . . The Bible is ascientific. . . . It does not speak unscientifically . . . nor does it speak antiscientifically. . . . It views Creation not from a theoretical or analytical vantage point but from a common experiential perspective. Biblical speech about the nature of the Creation is understandable in all ages because it comes in the language of ordinary human experience" (Howard J. Van Till in *The Fourth Day*, William B. Eerdmans Publishing Co., 1986).

If the Bible had been written in the language of ancient science, it would have been very inadequate for today. If it had been written in the language of modern science, it wouldn't have made any sense to people for thousands of years. But that doesn't mean Genesis is a myth. Nor does it mean that we can't discover scientific facts from what it suggests.

What it means is that we mustn't force the Genesis account to say more than it actually says. We can speculate about what different phrases hint at, but we have to be careful. Our claims may often reflect our interpretations and guesses.

What Do You Think?
Identifying Our Responses to the Debate

Distribute copies of Student Sheet 13, "Make Your Mark." Have kids fill out their sheets individually. Then let them make "live" reports as follows.

Before class, prepare five sheets of paper with a large numeral (1-5) on each. Tape these in order on a wall of your room, just above head level.

After kids complete Student Sheet 13, ask them to position themselves under the 1, 2, 3, 4, and 5 signs to show how they answered. Read a question and allow kids to locate themselves along the "wall continuum." Take a few minutes to discuss responses and the distribution of the group before going on to the next question. Note: If you think your group members would be too self-conscious to "take a stand" in this way, have a couple of students tally results from the sheet and announce them to the group.

If you plan to use Session 5, collect and save Student Sheet 13 questionnaires until then.

If you'll be using Session 3, explain that it will deal with eight arguments for evolution and some of the weaknesses in those claims. Close in prayer.

Did the Devil Make Darwin Do It?

That's the title of a book edited by David B. Wilson and published by Iowa State University. Wilson, an associate professor of history and mechanical engineering at Iowa State, felt the book was needed to refute the "alarming" rise of scientific creationism, both at the university and among the public at large. Even though three Iowa State faculty members had taught a course called "Creation: A Scientific Alternative in the Study of Origins," Wilson declares that real "scientists reject creationism.... They think that the Bible . . . does not provide scientific knowledge about the natural world."

But are the claims of evolution so completely conclusive? This session will acquaint your students with some of the reasons evolution must still be regarded as a theory and not as fact.

Is Evolution The Solution?

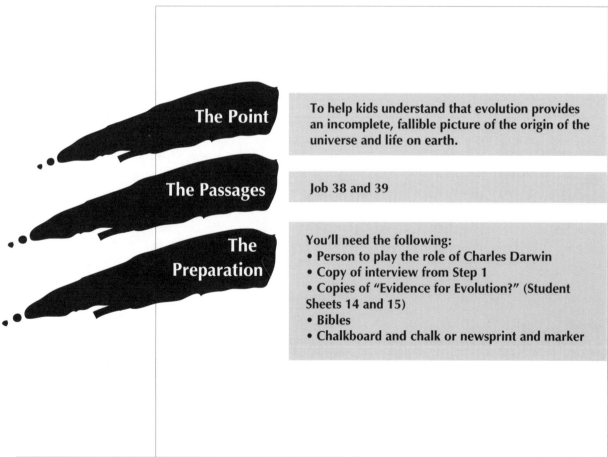

The Point	To help kids understand that evolution provides an incomplete, fallible picture of the origin of the universe and life on earth.
The Passages	Job 38 and 39
The Preparation	You'll need the following: • Person to play the role of Charles Darwin • Copy of interview from Step 1 • Copies of "Evidence for Evolution?" (Student Sheets 14 and 15) • Bibles • Chalkboard and chalk or newsprint and marker

Step 1

A Man and His Theory
Meeting the Man Who Popularized Evolution

Before the session, arrange to have an adult or teenager play the role of Charles Darwin. Costume isn't important. Just make sure the person has a copy of the following interview. When the session begins, bring "Darwin" up and start interviewing him.

Leader: Welcome to *Evolution Tonight.* Our guest is British naturalist Charles Darwin. Chuck, in 1859 you published a book called *The Origin of Species.* What was that all about?

Darwin: It said that all living things on earth descended, with changes, from a common ancestor. This is basically the theory of evolution. I wasn't the first person to suggest the idea, but I made a pretty impressive case in my book, if I say so myself. My book did more than anything else to gain widespread acceptance of the theory.

Leader: Fantastic. But something's been bothering me. I understand you used to be a Bible-quoting believer in God's special creation of each kind of life. Why would you write a book like this?

Darwin: I didn't set out to disprove the Genesis account of creation, if that's what you mean. But back in my day, most Christians felt you had to believe that the earth was only 6,000 years old—and that there was no change at all in plants and animals. When I sailed around the world on a ship called the *Beagle,* I saw some things that made me doubt this.

Leader: Like what?

Darwin: Oh, lots of geological wonders—deep canyons, towering mountains, enormous coral reefs—that I couldn't believe had been carved out or built up in only a few thousand years. And I saw evidence that species could change over time. That's how I came up with my theories, including the idea that change takes place through natural selection.

Leader: Great. And now most scientists seem to believe in your theory. Many even treat it as a proven fact. How do you feel about that?

Darwin: Uh. . . to tell you the truth, I'm not sure. By the time the last edition of my book was published in 1872, I wasn't so confident about my ideas. I couldn't answer many of my critics' questions. And I hadn't found those "missing links" my theory required—you know, fossils of animals that were halfway between one species and another. I predicted those gaps would be filled as more fossils were dug up. But now, 130 years later, those missing links are still missing.

Leader: Not to worry, Chuck. Your theories have been eagerly received by a world that wants explanations that don't require belief in God. Your ideas have gone from theory to fact without having to solve the problems you admitted. Congratulations!

Darwin: Uh, thanks . . . I guess.

After thanking your "Darwin," ask the group: **Did anything in this interview surprise you?**

What kinds of "proof" have you heard people give for evolution?

Let's review some of the evidence for evolution and see how strong it is.

Dusting for Fingerprints
Reviewing the Evidence for Evolution

Pass out copies of Student Sheets 14 and 15, "Evidence for Evolution?" These sheets address eight kinds of evidence for evolution frequently cited in biology textbooks.

Ask one student to read the claim for #1 and another to read the challenge. Follow with a discussion of kids' reactions before going on to the next area of evidence.

Go over as many of the eight areas as you have time for. Encourage kids to take the sheets with them after the session for later reference, when they are faced with claims like these.

Little Mike vs. Big Mac
Comparing Microevolution and Macroevolution

One of the main points of the information we just looked at was that a living thing may make dramatic changes within its kind—but can't necessarily evolve into a new kind. To illustrate this idea, let's try changing letters in a sentence and see what happens. (Note: This example is adapted from Michael Denton's *Evolution: a Theory in Crisis* [Adler and Adler, Publishers, Inc., 1985].)

Write the sentence, "He sat on the bed," on the chalkboard or newsprint. Ask kids to suggest possible variations that involve changing only one letter at a time. Each change must create a logical and grammatically correct sentence. Their efforts might look like the following.

> He sat on the bed.
> She sat on the bed.
> She sat in the bed.
> We sat on the bed.
> We sat in the bed.
> We sit in the bed.
> We sit on the bed.
> We sit on the beds.
> We sat on the beds.
> He sat in the bed.

If we changed bed to bid (as in delaying a financial transaction), we could get another set of variations. Bid could then be changed to bit (as in drill bit—it would be rather uncomfortable to sit on one, but logically and grammatically correct). Bed could also be changed to bud (as in flower bud).

But we run into problems if we try to evolve a bed into a chair. Write the following on the board or newsprint:

> He sat on the bed.
> He sat on the ced.
> He sat on the chd.
> He sat on the cha.
> He sat on the chai.
> He sat on the chair.

We can't go from "bed" to "chair" without passing through four steps that don't make sense on their own. You might call them "nonfunctional mutations," changes that don't work. That's the problem with evolving from one kind of living thing to another. Most of the in-between creatures couldn't survive.

A change in a living thing has to be an improvement—or at least not a handicap—for it to last.

Share the following example if you have time:

Take the supposed evolution of reptiles' scales into birds' feathers. There's no fossil evidence for such a change. But let's suppose, as evolutionists have suggested, that the scales on tree-climbing reptiles were stimulated to grow longer and longer by the friction of the air as they jumped from limb to limb. Finally the scales were frayed, and the fraying gradually became more and more featherlike until the first feather appeared.

The main problem with this theory is that even if long, lightweight scales helped a reptile jump, frayed scales would create "drag" and slow it down. Not until true feathers evolved would the animal gain any jumping advantage.

A feather has some similarity to a scale. But a feather has a unique design with parallel filaments that zip together like hooks and eyelets. Without that design you have nothing but a tangle that would catch on thorns and twigs, hindering the reptile's ability to move. How does this creature survive thousands of in-between years with a problem like that? Natural selection would get rid of such an animal.

So it's not only the missing links in the fossil record that weakens the theory of evolution. It's also the lack of believable bridges over those gaps.

Modesty and Honesty
Admitting Our Limits

Divide the group into pairs. Have partners take turns reading to each other as many verses as possible from Job 38 and 39. Then discuss:

Does God seem impressed with people's knowledge of how life and the universe came to be? (No.)

Why not? (None of us was there when He made the world.)

With our scientific knowledge today, can we answer the questions God asks here? (Not really. We may know more about the speed of light, for instance, but science can't tell us where light "comes from.")

As you close, avoid giving students the impression that the questions raised in this session prove that evolution is erroneous. The debate isn't that simple. Such a task, if it could be done, would require much more time. The purpose of this session is simply to demonstrate that evolutionary theory is not airtight and its truth is not self-evident. It has its problems, which Darwin readily admitted even if some modern evolutionists don't. And there are alternative explanations that have logical merit—as students will see if you use Session 4.

"Generations come and generations go, but the earth remains forever. The sun rises and the sun sets, and hurries back to where it rises. The wind blows to the south and turns to the north; round and round it goes, ever returning on its course. All streams flow into the sea, yet the sea is never full. To the place the streams come from, there they return again. All things are wearisome, more than one can say" (Ecclesiastes 1:4-8).

Carl Sagan portrayed the universe in much the same way in his TV series, *Cosmos.* "This is all there is and was and ever will be," he said. Such a mechanistic view leads many to a sense of futility and despair. If there is no Creator, no beginning, no end, no accountability, then what's the point of living?

This session is designed to introduce your kids to theories that reconcile science and Scripture. In doing so, you may also be guiding them to a sense of meaning and purpose in life.

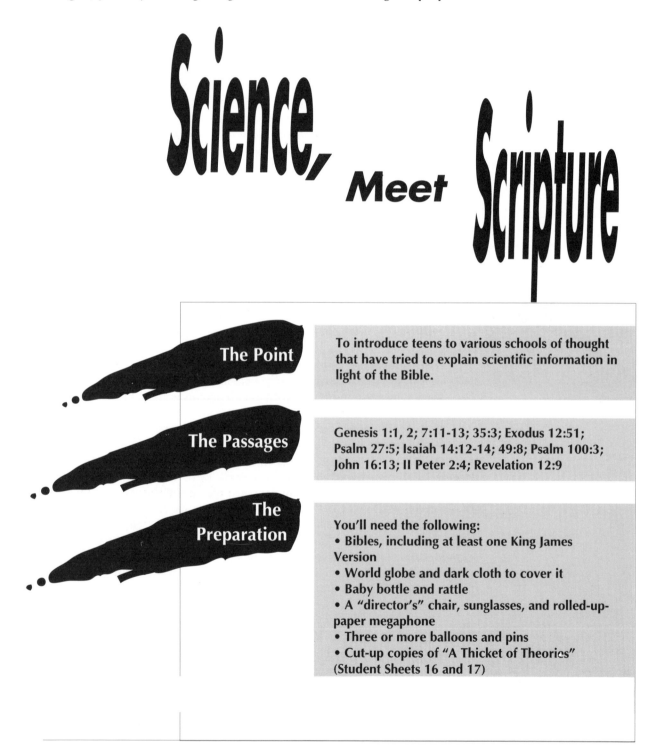

Science, Meet Scripture

The Point

To introduce teens to various schools of thought that have tried to explain scientific information in light of the Bible.

The Passages

Genesis 1:1, 2; 7:11-13; 35:3; Exodus 12:51; Psalm 27:5; Isaiah 14:12-14; 49:8; Psalm 100:3; John 16:13; II Peter 2:4; Revelation 12:9

The Preparation

You'll need the following:
• Bibles, including at least one King James Version
• World globe and dark cloth to cover it
• Baby bottle and rattle
• A "director's" chair, sunglasses, and rolled-up-paper megaphone
• Three or more balloons and pins
• Cut-up copies of "A Thicket of Theories" (Student Sheets 16 and 17)

No Business Like Show Business
Getting Ready to Look at Various Theories of Creation

We're going to do things a little differently today: You're going to do most of the leading! And I've got some strange objects to help you get your points across.

Form four teams (or use individuals if the group is small). Team 1 gets a world globe and a dark cloth big enough to cover it; Team 2 gets a baby bottle and rattle; Team 3 gets a folding canvas "director's" chair, a pair of sunglasses, and a piece of paper to roll up and use as a megaphone; and Team 4 gets at least three balloons and straight pins.

Before the session, copy and cut apart "A Thicket of Theories" (Student Sheets 16 and 17). Now give each team member a copy of the information needed to present its theory.

Explain that you're going to look at four ways in which people have tried to fit together scientific evidence and the Bible's account of creation. Each team, following the instructions on its part of the student sheet, will explain one of the four theories.

Give teams a few minutes to read their instructions and plan their presentations. Then, in the following order, have teams show each other what the four theories are all about.

The Land before Time
Understanding the Theory of a Pre-Genesis Earth

Have Team 1 present "The Land before Time"—the theory that there was a "pre-Genesis" world.

Then discuss the theory, using the following comments and questions as needed.

There are passages which can be used to support this theory, though their interpretation isn't certain. Ask a volunteer to read Isaiah 14:12-14 in a King James Version of the Bible. Ask other volunteers to read II Peter 2:4 and Revelation 12:9 (no specific version).

Do you think these verses support the "Land before Time" theory? Why or why not?

One possible problem with the theory is that the fossils from the "pre-Genesis world" are like the plants and animals living today. Did God copy preexisting forms? Did they all not die when the "pre-Genesis" world was devastated?

Another question: Did God use a collision with a meteor or comet to destroy Satan's domain? There's strong geologic evidence that the earth has been hit with massively destructive meteors in the distant past. But this evidence points to many such disasters over the history of the earth, not just one.

It's a Young World after All?
Explaining "Scientific Creationism"

Have Team 2 present "It's a Young World after All"—the theory that the world is no more than 10,000 years old.

Then discuss the theory, using the following comments as needed.

Creationists who believe in a young earth also point to the law of entropy (EN-truhpee). This law states that a closed system always decays into simpler and more chaotic parts—instead of developing the greater order and complexity required by evolution. This fits well with the claim that God created all life during six days of creation. Since then the world has been running down; many creatures have become extinct and some have varied (within their gene potentials), but none has evolved into a new and higher kind, they say.

There's just one problem. It's true that the universe as a whole is running down, but the case can be made that the earth is not a closed system. It continually has energy pumped into it from the sun. So, say the critics of this idea, earth's life forms do have the resources for improving.

What strengths do you see in the "young earth" theory?

What weaknesses do you see?

The Cosmic Director

Describing the Nonconsecutive-Literal-Days Theory

Have Team 3 present "The Cosmic Director"—the theory that God injected His "direction" into the creation process on six widely separated days.

Then discuss the theory, using the following questions as needed.

What makes sense to you about this theory?

What doesn't make sense?

Does the "cosmic director" idea fit your mental picture of God as Creator? Do you think it fits the biblical account?

The Big Bang

Examining Theistic Evolution

Have Team 4 present "The Big Bang"—the theory that God used evolution to create life and the universe.

Then discuss the theory, using the following verses, comments, and questions as needed.

Have volunteers look up the following verses: Genesis 7:11-13; 35:3; Exodus 12:51; Psalm 27:5; Isaiah 49:8. **Which of these verses seem to be talking about 24-hour days?** (Genesis 7:11-13; Exodus 12:51.)

Which could be talking about longer periods? (Genesis 35:3; Psalm 27:5; Isaiah 49:8.)

How is theistic evolution different from atheistic evolution? (A possibility: Atheistic evolutionists see the universe as an eternal machine with no end, no beginning, and therefore in no need of a Creator.)

While not buying all the theories of evolution, people like astrophysicist Howard Van Till are not shaken by evidence supporting evolution. They see it as the expression of God's strategy for the development of the universe.

What do you think of the idea that God used some kind of evolution to form life and the universe?

Playing Favorites
Responding to Theories of Creation

Thank the teams for their presentations and regather the whole group.

Which of these theories seems to be most fully accepted in our church? In your family? By you? Why?

Are there parts of various theories you'd put together?

Ask a volunteer to read John 16:13. **Does this mean that God will show you which of these theories is right?** (He could. But He might also choose to let you wait until you get to heaven to know all the answers.)

Here's one truth God has clearly revealed about the beginning of the world. Have group members look up Psalm 100:3. If possible, read it together.

Close with silent prayer, giving kids a chance to tell God how they feel about the fact that He created them—and to ask Him questions they may have about that process.

Jay, 16, loves a good argument. Sometimes he takes an opposing view just for the sake of an interesting discussion. So when Grandpa makes a comment about "godless evolution destroying the minds of the young," Jay jumps in with news of scientific discoveries that seem to support evolution. After a few minutes, Grandpa huffs: "Well, my Bible says that God created the earth in six days—and if you don't believe that, you might as well not call yourself a Christian!"

Later, Jay is talking with a classmate about various theories of origins. Jay expresses his opinion that it isn't so important how the beginning happened, but that God was the One who designed and planned it. The classmate sneers and says, "You believe that? I thought you were more intelligent. Nobody believes God created the earth out of nothing—except a bunch of ignorant fanatics!"

Do your kids ever feel like Jay—caught in the crossfire of the debate between creation and evolution? This session could help them.

Caught in the Crossfire

The Point	To help students become secure in their faith that God made the universe, and to help them act in a godly way toward those who disagree.
The Passages	Ephesians 4:11-15; Hebrews 11:3; Colossians 1:16; I John 3:13, 14; Titus 3:1, 2; I Timothy 1:3-5; 6:3-5
The Preparation	You'll need the following: • Bibles • Copies of "Talking Back" (Student Sheet 18) • New copies of "Make Your Mark" (Student Sheet 13, from Session 2) • Chalkboard and chalk or newsprint and marker • Pens or pencils • "Loaner" copies of some of the books listed in Step 4 (optional)

Firing Line
Responding to Others Who Have Strong Opinions

Pass out Student Sheet 18, "Talking Back." Have kids follow the instructions individually. If time allows, kids can write responses to more than three statements.

When most of the kids are done writing, read the statements one at a time and ask volunteers to read their responses. Assure students that responses may agree or disagree with the statements, depending on the student's opinion. As you discuss responses, you may want to make suggestions like these for kids who *disagree* with the statements:

1. You could point out some ways in which the Bible differs from other writings (fulfilled prophecies, many different authors whose writings fit together, etc.). You could also ask the person to consider whether the Bible's account makes sense. And you could mention that the existence of so many creation stories means that people want to know where they came from; it doesn't have to mean all explanations are equally valid.

2. You could say that people like Darwin came up with the theory of evolution to try to explain what they observed—not necessarily to destroy faith. You might also point out that kids need to know about a theory so many people believe, or that both sides may not be heard if all the Christians pull out of classes.

3. You could note that science can't answer the question of whether God exists.

4. See point 3, "Embryology," on Student Sheet 14, "Evidence for Evolution?" (used in Session 3).

5. You could mention some of the interpretations people have of the Genesis account (see Session 4).

6. You could note that some scientists with no particular religious beliefs have begun questioning evolutionary theory. And it works both ways; some people start with a belief in evolution and try to bend evidence to fit it. Each "side" needs to listen carefully to the other.

7. You could agree that the most important thing *is* that God did it—but that it's also important to take the Genesis account seriously if the rest of the Bible is to be taken seriously.

Which of these words describes the approach you think you should take when you disagree with someone about creation and evolution: Fighting, insulting, arguing, discussing, or avoiding?

Which of these approaches is easiest for you to take? Which is hardest? Why?

The Bottom Line
Using Scripture to Discover What's Most Important

Before the session, write the following references on chalkboard or newsprint. Now assign individuals to read the passages silently. Be sure each student is assigned at least one passage.

Ephesians 4:11-16
Hebrews 11:3
Colossians 1:16
I John 3:13, 14
Titus 3:1-2

I Timothy 1:3-5
I Timothy 6:3-5

As kids read, they should ask themselves, "How could this Scripture apply to the 'Great Debate' between creation and evolution?"

When kids have had time to find and reflect on their assigned passages, ask them to read their verses aloud and answer the question they were to ask themselves. Do this for each of the Scripture passages.

Then ask students what principles from the verses stand out as most important in the debate between creation and evolution. Encourage free discussion, but draw out or add some of the following observations:

- It is by faith that we believe in God and the works of His hands.
- Creation is not only by God but for God.
- When we talk about these things we should speak the truth in love.
- Having a "correct" doctrine about creation isn't what saves a person. Faith in Christ saves, and having God's love for one another shows that we belong to the Lord.
- There is a danger of the issue becoming more important than loving those with whom we disagree.
- We need to study enough not to have our faith shaken by teachings that do not acknowledge God as the source of our life and our faith.

If you have time, ask students which of the Scriptures they've just read might be helpful in responding to statements on Student Sheet 18.

The Windup
Summing Up What's Been Learned

If you've used the rest of the sessions in this unit, try a review. Pass out fresh copies of "Making Your Mark" (Student Sheet 13). Have kids read through the questions once more. Encourage them to mark where they are now on each scale and compare it to their original mark (if they can remember their earlier responses).

Have some of your thoughts and feelings changed as a result of these sessions? How and why? Have some stayed the same or been strengthened?

Encourage feedback on what's been most helpful—or unhelpful—about these sessions. If kids have concerns that haven't been addressed, steer them toward some of the books listed in Step 4.

Pray together for grace to respond with patience, courage, and love toward those who have different views of creation and evolution. Ask God for wisdom to speak the truth in love. Thank Him for His love in creating the world with all its wonders, and for creating humans to be in fellowship with Him.

Extra Credit (optional)
Exploring Further Information about Creation and Evolution

If possible, choose a few of the following books and make them available to group members who would like to further explore the creation/evolution issue:

It's a Young World After All by Paul D. Ackerman (Baker Book House, 1986). This book looks at many of the nonbiological arguments for a young earth.

Evolution: A Theory in Crisis by Michael Denton (Adler and Adler, Publishers, Inc., 1985). This scholarly book reviews many of the problems with the theory of evolution.

Evolution: The Fossils Say No! by Duane T. Gish (Creation Life Publishers, 1973). Focusing primarily on paleontology, Gish claims that there is no more support for evolution from the past than from the present.

Scientific Creationism by Henry M. Morris (Creation Life Publishers, 1974). The director of the Institute for Creation Research presents scientific creationism and attempts to refute evolution—as well as critiquing theories other than scientific creationism that try to take the Bible seriously.

Creation: The Facts of Life by Gary Parker (Creation Life Publishers, 1980). A former evolutionist provides an easy-to-understand overview of scientific creationism.

It Couldn't Just Happen by Lawrence O. Richards (Word, 1988). This book surveys relevant fields of science and asserts that the weight of scientific evidence is on the side of creationism.

How to Think About Evolution and Other Bible Science Controversies by Duane Thurman (InterVarsity Press, 1978). Looking at all sides of the question, Thurman attempts to clear the emotional fog and expose hidden sources of conflict.

The Fourth Day by Howard Van Till (William B. Eerdmans Publishing Co., 1986). Astrophysicist Van Till argues that neither the biblical nor the scientific description of the cosmos is complete in itself.

Did the Devil Make Darwin Do It? David B. Wilson, editor (Iowa State University Press, 1983). While not very sympathetic to Christianity, this book details the claims of evolutionists who are incensed over creationism.

Mrs. Huntington

Farley, the butler, has just found your dead son by the fireplace in the ballroom of your home, Huntington Manor. He was your only child and a great comfort in your old age. Some say it was suicide, others an accident or sudden physical collapse (even though he was only 18). But the constable thinks it was murder. How can they all be so concerned about the cause? All you care about is that he is gone and you are alone. Talk of anything else is an insult to his memory and ignores your great grief.

Constable McDoogle

You have just been called to the Huntington estate where Farley, the butler, has found M. R. Huntington, Esquire, dead. There is no obvious wound, and under the body—which lay by the fireplace in the ballroom—you discovered a "suicide" note stating: "I just can't take it any more. Please forgive me." But you don't believe the death was by suicide. You suspect Farley of murder because he once told you that he was listed in the will as an heir to the estate—after young Mr. Huntington, of course. You're intent on nabbing Farley quick.

Farley

You have been the butler at Huntington Manor for the past 33 years. Only the old man really appreciated you. Before his death ten years ago, he even wrote you into his will—after young M.R., of course. But this morning you found the 18-year-old master of the house dead in the ballroom. You could see no obvious cause for his death. Thinking of how much you had to gain by his death—and fearing that people might suspect you had a hand in it—you wrote a suicide note and slipped it under his body.

Mildred Walters

You have been the maid at Huntington Manor for over a year. But maybe it was a mistake. You've been in love with young M.R. since childhood, but he paid you little attention even though you lived just down the lane. You hoped that if you could be near him every day, he couldn't help but notice you. Instead, he came to scorn you as beneath him. You began to understand why they say love is so close to hate. Both of those feelings have swirled out of control in your heart. But now M.R. is dead, and you feel like leaving Huntington Manor.

No Big Deal?

On August 6, 1945, a U.S. Army plane dropped a single atomic bomb on the center of Hiroshima, Japan. It killed more than 92,000 people and destroyed 4.7 square miles of the city. "It was necessary," some said.

Shortly after midnight on March 23, 1989, the supertanker *Exxon Valdez* ran aground on the rocks in Alaska's Prince William Sound. At the bridge of his ship, Captain Joseph Hazelwood reportedly turned to his chief mate and said, "Well, it's one way to end a career." Before the rupture in the 987-foot-long vessel could be plugged, 240,000 barrels of crude oil had created the worst oil-spill disaster in North American waters.

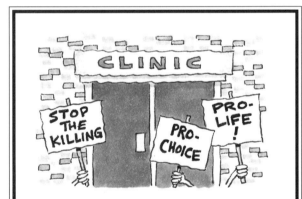

The number of abortions conducted in the United States between 1973 and 1989 equaled the populations of Montana, North Dakota, South Dakota, Colorado, Wyoming, Iowa, Nebraska, Utah, New Mexico, Oklahoma, and Kansas. Surveys show that 95 percent of the abortions were done for "social reasons." Only 1 percent were conducted for reasons of incest or rape. Some say of the decision to have an abortion, "It's my business—nobody else's."

In April 1989 a gang in New York City attacked, beat, and raped a woman as she was jogging through Central Park. When the gang was arrested and was asked the reason for the crime, one member said: "It was fun."

Most scientists agree that there are basic, natural laws that govern how matter and energy act all over the explored universe. That doesn't mean scientists think they understand or have even discovered all the laws of nature. But they believe the universe abides by such laws.

Not everyone agrees that today's natural laws have always been in effect exactly as we now see them. So there are three types of explanations of how things began:

1. **Those that use only natural laws.**
2. **Those that use unnatural laws (suggesting that at one time the laws of nature were different).**
3. **Those using supernatural laws (suggesting that a Creator shaped the universe).**

Where Did Those Rings Come From?

Evolutionary scientists claim to use only natural laws—dealing only in what they can observe or can reasonably conclude from observing. For instance, when they see that trees add one ring of growth each year, they conclude that a tree with 400 rings is 400 years old—even if no human recorded the tree's existence 400 years ago.

These scientists would say it's possible that something not yet seen caused the tree to add ten rings per year, making it only 40 years old (an unnatural law); or that God created the tree a week ago with all 400 rings in place (a supernatural law). But these scientists don't think there's sufficient reason to adopt those ideas. Such explanations, they say, can't be tested or worked with in a laboratory.

God: Yes, No, or Maybe?

Some who believe in evolution combine it with a theory called "materialistic determinism." This theory holds that since we can't "test" for God's existence, there is no God and no free will; only material things are real. These people go beyond saying that they can't work with unnatural or supernatural laws; they say neither has ever occurred. They claim everything is a result of the blind activity of matter and energy.

Classic evolution and materialistic determinism have something in common: Neither uses God in its explanations. But materialistic determinism goes beyond observation. It makes claims that can't be tested or proven (one can't prove that there is no God, for example).

Many creationists think all evolutionists are also materialistic determinists. But that's not necessarily so. You might say that classic evolutionism is agnostic (says that God is unknown) while materialistic determinism is atheistic (says that there is no God.)

Make Your Mark

As you read the following questions, write an "x" on each scale to show your response. For example, on question A, if you're *almost* sure that 24-hour days are required, you'd make a mark between 1 and 2.

A. Do you feel an accurate view of Genesis 1 requires believing in six twenty-four-hour days of creation?

1_____2_____3_____4_____5
Definitely   Definitely not

B. How bothered are you by the seeming differences between the claims of science and the Bible concerning our beginnings?

1_____2_____3_____4_____5
Not disturbed   Very disturbed

C. Do you think there are believable explanations for our beginnings that harmonize the Bible's account and the findings of science?

1_____2_____3_____4_____5
Definitely   Definitely not

D. How "different" from teachers and students at school do you feel over the creation/evolution issue?

1_____2_____3_____4_____5
Not at all   A lot

E. How "different" from other Christians do you feel over the creation/evolution issue?

1_____2_____3_____4_____5
Not at all   A lot

Evidence for Evolution?

1. Paleontology

The claim of evolution: Paleontology, the study of fossils, proves that complex organisms evolved from simpler ones. A complete record of evolution hasn't been found in the fossil record, but older sedimentary rocks do tend to have more primitive fossils.

As for "missing links," how about the archeopteryx? We knew there must have been a creature halfway between reptiles and birds, since birds evolved from reptiles. Then the archeopteryx was found. The claws on its wings, teeth in its mouth, and longer than usual tail are decidedly "reptilian" features.

The challenge of creation: This example isn't so impressive. The fully developed feathers and wings of the archeopteryx, so well designed for flight, suggest that it was a full-fledged bird. If it were a true link, the wings would be only partly developed. As for teeth, some reptiles have them and some don't—and some other fossilized birds had teeth. And the modern ostrich has claws on its wings.

There's more than one possible explanation for fossils like the archeopteryx. They don't have to be ancestors of present plants and animals; they could be extinct cousins.

After more than 130 years of digging, there are now more *missing* links than ever. David Raup, curator of the Field Museum of Natural History in Chicago, has said that "some of the cases of Darwinian change in the fossil record, such as the evolution of the horse in North America, have had to be discarded or modified as a result of more detailed information."

2. Comparative Anatomy

The claim of evolution: Look at the many body parts that are similar in different kinds of mammals. For instance, the forelimbs of the human, the whale, the dog, and the bat are used for entirely different purposes and are of very different sizes—but their bone structure is basically similar. Doesn't this show a clear relationship to a common ancestor?

The challenge of creation: There could be another explanation for the similarities: Creation according to a common plan. The forelimbs of most mammals *are* similar, but they also resemble hindlimbs. If the human hand and foot evolved from the pectoral and pelvic fins of a fish, would both limbs develop five digits each? Why not six and three? Or five and one (like a hoof)? It's at least possible that the limbs are similar because the Creator used certain themes and variations—as human artists and engineers do.

Then there's the problem of "convergence." This happens when widely separated species on the evolutionist's "family tree" show up with very similar features. Take, for instance, the human eye and the eyes of squids and octopuses. They're remarkably similar. How can that be the result of evolution when these creatures are so far apart in the evolutionist's scheme of things? A Creator, on the other hand, could return to a familiar pattern at any point in His creation.

3. Embryology

The claim of evolution: The embryonic development of animals repeats that of their evolutionary ancestors. This shows their close relationship to each other. Parts of the embryo develop as though the creature were going to be a lower form of life—and then disappear.

If we haven't evolved, why does the human embryo develop useless "gill" slits like a fish, a "yolk sac" like a bird, and a "tail" like a lizard? If a Creator had made us, why wouldn't our embryonic development be more direct rather than taking these useless detours?

The challenge of creation: Good question—*if* those organs are truly useless. But they're not. The yolk sac is the only source for the embryo's first blood cells. Remove it, and the embryo dies. The "gill" slits got their name from their position, not their structure. They become the middle ear canal and the parathyroid and thymus glands. As for the misnamed "tail," our tailbone is the necessary connection for the muscles that enable us to stand up. It sticks out like a tail in the embryo only because the legs haven't yet developed to surround it.

4. Comparative Biochemistry

The claim of evolution: Hemoglobin is the protein found in the blood that carries oxygen to the cells. It appears in all vertebrates, and its structure is very similar among vertebrates that are closely related—mammals, for instance. This proves they're related by evolution.

The challenge of creation: Then we ought to be able to trace how hemoglobin evolved. But hemoglobin also is found here and there among invertebrates—like some earthworms, starfish, clams, and some insects. This doesn't seem to fit the evolutionary "tree." Could it be that instead of proving evolution, these similarities show the genius of a Creator who uses ingredients wherever they work best—much as a carpenter uses the same kind of nail to build a fence as he does to build a house?

Evidence for Evolution? *(cont.)*

5. Chromosome Structure

The claim of evolution: The more closely related two species appear to be, the more alike their chromosome structure is. For instance, the chromosome patterns of a chimpanzee and an orangutan are practically the same.

The challenge of creation: In most cases this is true. But this argument for evolution was seriously shaken when scientists discovered that *different* genes determine similar structures in different species. And within a species several different characteristics can be affected by one gene. For instance, changes in the gene that orders the development of a chicken's air sacs and downy feathers will also affect the lungs and kidneys, which occur in many other vertebrates.

6. Protective Resemblance

The claim of evolution: In the British Isles during the last century, the peppered moth was light colored with dark markings. Then in 1849 a black form of the moth was discovered near Manchester, England. By 1900 the darker moth was in the majority, and by the 1950's 98 percent of the moths were the darker kind.

Why? Pollution from coal smoke had killed the light-colored lichen (a plant) that grew on the trees where the moths perched. The light-colored moth, which had been perfectly camouflaged against the lichen, began to stand out on the dark bark of the trees. Predatory birds snapped up the light moths. But dark moths were able to perch on the now dark trees without being seen. Recently, as pollution control has improved, the lichen is regrowing and the light-colored moths are making a comeback.

This shows adaptive evolution at work—and quickly enough to be recorded. It seems to prove natural selection and the survival of the fittest.

The challenge of creation: Natural selection and the survival of the fittest on this small scale is not proof of evolution. The original moths had dark pigment in their genes and some variety in their coloring. The darker moths stayed alive long enough to reproduce, while the light ones were gobbled up. Ranchers can produce color changes in animals, too—by selective breeding. A moth or a sheep that changes color isn't necessarily on its way to becoming a new kind of animal. It's still a moth or a sheep.

7. Geographical Distribution

The claim of evolution: About 600 miles off the coast of South America are a group of islands called the Galapagos. When Charles Darwin visited there he discovered 13 species of birds that have come to be known as "Darwin's finches." While different from each other in size, plumage, beak design, and behavior, they were all finches.

If creation is the correct explanation of origins, these birds must have migrated to the islands from mainland continents. But none of these finches is found anywhere else in the world. They must have evolved from a common ancestor that migrated to the islands eons ago—thus proving the process of evolution.

The challenge of creation: The issue here is the difference between microevolution (changes within one kind) and macroevolution (one kind of animal changing into another).

The genes of the finch contained many adaptive variations. Certain features could become dominant as the environment demanded (as with the peppered moth). This might be called microevolution. But no real improvement occurred that wasn't already possible in the genes. No macroevolution brought about a truly new "kind."

Gary Parker says in his book, *Creation: the Facts of Life* (CLP Publishers, 1980) that "natural selection works only because each created kind was endowed, by plan and purpose at creation, with sufficient variety to multiply and fill the earth in all its ecologic and geographic variety."

8. Domestication

The claim of evolution: For thousands of years people have been breeding plants and animals to "improve" them (to come up with a type of corn that resists disease, for instance). Dramatic changes have occurred. In rare instances a new species is developed—if one defines a species as an actual or potential interbreeding organism that doesn't interbreed with others.

We know such significant change can take place. The only thing required to explain the evolution of *all* living things from a single source is sufficient time and opportunity (through natural selection).

The challenge of creation: Even though a certain degree of microevolution can and does occur, that doesn't mean unlimited change is possible. The fact that many plants and animals are extinct could suggest that they couldn't make major changes in order to survive. There are limits to microevolution, and those limits are found in the creatures' genetic potentials.

A Thicket of Theories

Team 1: The Land before Time

Here are the instructions for your presentation.

Read Genesis 1:1, 2 aloud to the whole group. Then, if you have a globe and cloth as props, cover and uncover the globe with the cloth as noted while you share the following information.

The first theory says that these verses are talking about an ancient creation of the earth [uncover globe]. After that, millions of years may have passed while plants and animals lived and died, laying down fossils in much the same way geologists would describe.

But this "early earth" was the domain of Lucifer (Satan), the star of the morning. He ruled it until he tried to be equal with God. God then cast him and his accomplice angels down. Earth also suffered as a result of this judgment, becoming "formless and empty" with "darkness over the surface of the deep" [cover globe].

God might have used a collision with a meteor or comet to destroy Satan's domain. That could have caused the dark and chaos described in Genesis 1:2—much like the "nuclear winter" scientists warn us about.

As time passed, light was probably refracted by the dirt and dust in the atmosphere. There probably wasn't much distinction between day and night [read Genesis 1:3 out loud]. As more dust fell and the sky began to clear, there would be less refraction. Light [uncover globe] would become separated from the darkness [read Genesis 1:4 out loud]. Finally, the sun and moon would be visible enough "to mark seasons and days and years" [read Genesis 1:14 out loud].

Whether or not evolution was the means by which life developed before this time of chaos is not important, since Genesis does not describe that period.

According to this theory, God—who so often brings good out of bad—brought new life to the world as Genesis describes.

Team 2: It's a Young World after All

Here are the instructions for your presentation.

If you have a baby bottle and rattle or other props, use them as you share the following information. Your team could also begin by singing, "It's a Young World after All," to the tune of "It's a Small World after All."

One of the most popular theories among creation scientists these days is the "young earth" model. Creationists used to say the earth was about 6,000 years old, a figure they got by adding up the ages of people mentioned in the Bible's family histories. But now it's recognized that the Bible doesn't necessarily account for every generation, though it seems to mention most of them. So some creationists assume a maximum age of about 10,000 years—not millions or billions of years as other scientists do.

These creationists accept a literal, six-day creation. They say the world had certain appearances of age from the moment of creation. This was not a trick by God to make it look older; it was necessary. For instance, soil appears to be rock eroded over great periods of time—but soil was required at the beginning for plants. And soil wouldn't stay on hillsides unless it was held there by roots from trees, shrubs, and grass—all suggesting age.

These scientists don't suggest that God created the fossils within the rocks, though. Fossils, they say, were the result of the flood of Noah's time. This flood, they say, filled up great hollows with silt and the carcasses of dead animals.

They point to huge fossil beds, where the bones of dinosaurs lie like heaps of toothpicks—suggesting something like a flood as the cause. Otherwise, why would so many die at the same time in the same place? It's only in unusual circumstances of burial—like a mud slide or a huge flood—that a fossil has a chance to form.

But why do fossils of simple organisms appear in lower layers of rock, while more complex animals appear in upper layers? "Young earth" creationists point out that the complete set of fossils from simple to complex isn't found in any one place. They suggest that a fossil's location reflects the environment in which the animal lived. In a book called *Creation: The Facts of Life* (Creation Life Publishers), Gary Parker writes: "A walk through Grand Canyon, then, is not like a walk through evolutionary time; instead, it's like a walk from the bottom of the ocean, across the tidal zone, over the shore, across the lowlands, and on into the upland regions."

In support of this, "young earth" creationists point to "misplaced" fossils—fossils in lower layers that shouldn't have appeared until much later according to evolution. For instance, the Castenedolo and Olmo human skulls (found in Italy) were uncovered in layers well below the one in which "modern" man is said to have developed.

Team 3: The Cosmic Director

Here are the instructions for your presentation.

If you have the following props, choose a "director" to be your spokesperson. That person should wear the sunglasses and sit in the director's chair. Roll up the paper for the director to use as a megaphone. The rest of your team can act as crew or cast members on a movie set as the director shares the following.

Just as a film director must prompt the actors to move on to the next scene, the "nonconsecutive literal days" theory suggests that God periodically injected nature with His creative direction.

According to this theory, God performed instant acts of creation on each of the six days of creation, just as the Bible says. But the days may have been separated by enormous periods of time—time when the fossils could have been laid down.

This theory doesn't try to allow for evolution. But it does try to allow for the fossils that many scientists say took millions of years to form. And it still interprets Genesis in a literal way.

Recently some evolutionists have tried to explain the lack of "missing links" in the fossil record by suggesting that evolution occurred in jumps separated by long periods of relative stability. The "cosmic director" theory is a little like that; it explains that the "jumps" happened because God stepped in to give "directions" on six critical days.

Team 4: The Big Bang

Here are the instructions for your presentation.

Appoint a spokesperson to share the information on this theory. The other members of your team should blow up at least three balloons (if you have them) and hold onto them (and some straight pins) until instructed to use them.

You might call this theory "The Big Bang." [Pop one of the balloons.] It's one explanation using theistic evolution—the idea that God used some kind of evolutionary development to form life and the universe.

The theory uses a non-literal reading of Genesis, which means that some of the words are interpreted as figures of speech. The six days of creation are taken as six long periods of time. Those who agree with this idea point out that the word translated "day" in Genesis 1 does not always mean a literal 24-hour period.

In Genesis 1 each act of creation begins with, "And God said . . . " and ends with, "And God saw that it was good." These seem to be poetic ways of writing, leading some to think that the verses should be treated more as poetry than as scientific information. They say the verses are like a reading in a worship service, emphasizing God as the Creator and the goodness of His creation. These are the most important parts in the passage, they say; if we try to read the verses from a scientific perspective, we miss the point.

Many of those who hold this theory would probably say that the Bible is reliable—but that different passages should be interpreted in different ways.

Theistic evolutionists tend to be interested in scientific discoveries that support the biblical claim that God is Creator. For instance, most have been happy about the evidence for the "Big Bang" theory of the origin of the universe [pop another balloon]. The universe seems to be expanding, with the rate of expansion slowing down. Some scientists say this shows there must have been a violent cosmic explosion [pop any balloons you may have left] at one point in space billions of years ago, from which was flung all matter and energy. That could suggest, or at least allow for, a Creator.

Talking Back

Choose three of the following statements—especially those that come close to ones you've heard people make. Then write a possible response to each.

MUSEUM OF NATURAL HISTRIONICS

1. "How do you know that what the Bible says about creation is true? All cultures have some story or myth about how the world was created!"

2. "Evolution is a teaching of the devil, and Christians should pull their kids out of classes where it is taught."

3. "Evolution proves there is no God. Humans are the highest developmental form."

4. Question on a high school science test: "How do the gill slits on a human embryo demonstrate evolution?"

5. "If you don't believe God created the world in six days like the Bible says, you can't be a Christian."

6. "People who believe in so-called creation science are starting with a religious belief and then trying to bend science to fit into it."

7. "It doesn't matter how the earth was created. What matters is that God did it."

How to Talk to Kids about Temptation

by Barry St. Clair

Every day I'm tempted. You are, too. It's definitely an area in which you can identify with your students.

Professional speakers will tell you that having experienced what you're talking about gives you a greater degree of understanding of your topic and your audience. No problem there with temptation. This topic never goes away. We will always face temptation. James said, *"When* tempted. . . " (James 1:13) It faces you, like it faces me, every day.

The advantage: You know temptation pulls at you on a very personal level. The disadvantage: Maybe you're giving in to temptation in an area of your life. It may be dragging on you as much as it is on the kids in your group—maybe more.

You First

The problem is that we have to *speak with integrity.* And many of us—let's be honest—haven't mastered temptation. If you've conquered lust and anger, what about ambition, greed, or jealousy? If you're walking in victory over fantasizing, have you also conquered materialism and fear?

I won't give you five steps to revival right now (read *Fireseeds of Spiritual Awakening* by Dan Hayes for that), but hang with me for a few paragraphs. Use this opportunity for God to search out your life and to press on along the trail of holiness.

You can never fully escape temptation; the question is how you handle it. You don't have to be perfect, just in the process. Are you pursuing holiness, integrity, purity—or are you giving in?

Are you disappointed? I'm supposed to be telling you how to talk with kids about temptation, and it feels like I'm nailing you. You're right, I am—because nothing discredits your message more than a lack of personal integrity. And nothing injects more vitality and spiritual power into your message than personal holiness. Nothing.

I'm not just talking about spiritual, unseen results, though they are very present and real. Right now I'm talking about a basic principle of life: You can't lead someone for long beyond your current level of experience.

There won't be any conviction or certainty in your message until you've lived it. Principles you've heard from others don't carry any weight in your mind until they're lived out in your life. And if they don't carry any weight with you, imagine how they'll come across to your kids.

Okay, time out. You get the point. Are you tired out yet? Now we're getting to the part you came for.

Now It's Their Turn

For talking to kids on a group level or one-to-one, I do have a few suggestions. First, *speak from your experience.* Don't pretend you're detached from the topic. This can make kids feel you're so holy that to get to be like you will take too long. It can make them feel hopeless. It can also set you up as the failure-free "minister" (with the appropriate angelic chorus accompanying the mention of that word), setting you apart from them. They can't relate to someone perfect. You want to be set apart from sin, not from your kids.

Sharing your fight against temptations can have a great impact on your kids. If you're willing to be honest and approachable with them, you'll be able to affect them much more. Your faith-testing encounters with temptation will help them see you as a fellow struggler in the faith. Your honesty will help them identify with you. Your example will inspire them and motivate them rather than defeat them. Give them hope that victory is possible.

But let the response be theirs. Love them, live out your life before them, be honest with them, and challenge them to holiness. Then leave the response to the Holy Spirit and to them. Otherwise, you run the risk of trying to manipulate your kids for a reaction.

Use discretion as you share your struggles with them. You don't have to tell kids the details of a particular area, but don't shy away from honesty, either.

Talk about direct issues in kids' lives. Kids aren't crying and dying to hear you talk about temptation. They won't queue up to hear even a *great* talk on temptation. But they will when it addresses the area in which *they're* facing temptation.

Announcing that you're going to tell kids "all about temptation" is like a teacher saying she's going to "cover the material" in class. But if she says she's going to hold a study session before a test, and everyone who attends is guaranteed at least a passing grade because she won't leave until she's sure every last person understands—that's another story. Let me put it this way: Can you imagine the line for tickets if the Beatles announced a reunion tour, including John Lennon? She'll see kids she hasn't seen all term!

Talking about your kids' concerns doesn't mean you have to touch on just one area of temptation. You can hit many. But talk about specifics, not about temptation in general. Talk about the benefits of resisting temptation, too.

Identify the source of temptation. Cover this in the way your church accepts, but let kids know there's someone working against them. The devil didn't "make me do it"—James assured early Christians that their "own evil desire" (1:14) did the job—but the enemy can offer a lot of ideas and try to make life miserable.

One caution, however: Let kids know that the real issue is how they respond to the temptations the enemy throws at them. They can't escape personal responsibility for the outcome of any temptation. God knows the devil well, and even He's not going to accept excuses blaming the devil for sin when your kids stand before Him.

Helping kids understand temptation is great. But you want them to resist temptation, to stand strong against it. *Offer students solutions when you talk about temptation.* Talk in terms of practical, step-by-step strategies to deal with it.

How have you overcome temptation? Look at your struggles and see if you notice a pattern. It's fine if you don't; but you might, and it could provide the basis for a strong message. Your steps in overcoming can help kids. You can say, "Hey, this really works!"

If you're able to handle temptation in most areas of your life, you've probably learned the value of having someone hold you accountable. There's a compelling force in knowing that someone will be asking about your obedience in the last day or week, in specifics. *Tell kids about the power of accountability.*

Your students need to know that the struggle against sin resulting from temptation will be lifelong. *Prepare them for the long, winding road.* Resisting some temptations may require a lot of work and take some time. Others may disappear almost immediately under the pressure of concerted effort. Again, your experience may be used to illustrate this.

Most of all, *emphasize the power of God in kids' lives to overcome temptation.* Your group members who are Christians never face temptation alone. God won't tempt them, but He will stand beside them. He gives them His Holy Spirit to bring Scripture to mind, to guide them to righteousness, and to convict them of specific sin when they start to turn away.

"Because he [Jesus] himself suffered when he was tempted, he is able to help those who are being tempted" (Hebrews 2:18). "And God is faithful; he will not let you be tempted beyond what you can bear. But when you are tempted, he will also provide a way out so that you can stand up under it" (I Corinthians 10:13).

Talking about temptation gives you a chance to let kids in on your life. If you're prepared, don't be surprised if you inspire them to tackle *their* temptations.

Barry St. Clair, once a teenager himself, has worked with students since his college days (and don't ask when that was). He has spoken to hundreds of thousands along the way. He founded Reach Out Ministries, a group serving youth leaders around the world. He has written many books for leaders and students, including Dating: Picking (and Being) a Winner, *and* Sex: Desiring the Best *(both from Here's Life Publishers).*

TEMPTATION

by Chris Frear

Chris Frear is a copywriter for Walk Thru the Bible Ministries in Atlanta, Georgia. Formerly communications director for Reach Out Ministries, Chris has worked with young people for more than five years. He and his wife have a growing youth ministry of their own at home—two preschool "pre-teens."

Resisting temptation is easier said than done. Kids know that as well as anyone does. For years adults have been looking at the symptoms of teenage temptation and telling kids to "just say no." That may get some kids to change certain behaviors, but it doesn't reach kids at the *source* of their temptations.

In this session, you'll begin showing kids a strategy for understanding and handling temptation—a strategy that may even help them root out embedded habits.

It will take time for kids to apply what they learn in this session. But if they do, you may see them set free to start ministering to one another. And since temptation affects all of us, you might even teach *yourself* something along the way.

Why Is Sin So Much Fun?

The Point

To help kids understand the dynamics of temptation—why its draw is so powerful and why the results usually seem fun, at least for a while.

The Passages

Jeremiah 17:5, 7; I Peter 5:8, 9; I John 4:4

The Preparation

You'll need the following:
• Chalkboard and chalk or newsprint and marker
• Pens or pencils
• Bibles
• Copies of "Do the Right Thing?" (Student Sheet 19)
• Copies of "You Need What?" (Student Sheet 20)
• Lightweight paper bag and milk carton filled with water
• Large pan

Do Sinners Have More Fun?
Facing the Fact That Sin Is Usually Attractive

If possible, start by telling the group about a time when you gave in to temptation and it felt good—at least for a while. For example, you might have slyly put down someone who embarrassed you in conversation.

Then pass out copies of Student Sheet 19, "Do the Right Thing?"

Maybe you've heard of a movie called, *Do the Right Thing*. But in life, sometimes it seems more fun to "Do the Wrong Thing." Here are a few situations for you to think about. Try to picture yourself in each one and write how you'd feel if you were in it. Be honest. You won't have to read your responses aloud if you don't want to.

After about five minutes, read the first situation from the sheet. Ask volunteers to read their responses. If they need help getting started, you could share honestly (or humorously) how you would feel.

Once you've heard at least one response for each scenario, say something like this: **For most of us, sin can seem satisfying, fun, or at least like the best choice at the time. Why do you think that is?**

Some kids may give "proper" theological responses (Our sinful nature influences us, etc.), but others may not feel the behaviors on the student sheet should be called sins (It's really not bad; the other person deserves it, etc.)

Here's an idea. Maybe the actions on this sheet seem satisfying, fun, or best because they temporarily satisfy one of our basic needs or desires. That's not an excuse for doing the wrong thing. But if we're interested in doing more of the right thing, we need to look at those basic needs and desires.

Just the Needs, Ma'am
Searching for Our Basic Needs and Desires

Hand out copies of Student Sheet 20, "You Need What?" **Take a look at the items on this sheet. Identify each one as a need, a want, or a like. A need is something you can't live without; a want is something you wish to have but could live without; a like is something that appeals to you but that you don't necessarily feel you must own. For example, you *need* transportation. To fulfill the need, you could use a bike. But you *want* a car. You'd *like* a Porsche, but a used Chevy would be okay. Get the idea?**

Give kids a few minutes to write their answers. Then discuss the results. Try to reach consensus on what the real needs on the list are (probably friends, bed, water, place to live—plus school hot lunch and bus ride, if kids can't bring lunches to school and can't walk there.)

After you've identified needs, add two more: **Two of our most basic needs are *to be loved and accepted* and *to be important to others*. These are parts of our personalities that God built into us. He also gave us physical needs for things like food, water, and warmth—and basic desires for things like family, sexual intimacy, and belonging to a group. These are all good. It's how we go about satisfying those needs and desires that determines whether we're doing the right thing or the wrong.**

You Get What You Need
Comparing Ways to Meet Needs and Basic Desires

Step 3

Referring to the needs on Student Sheet 20, plus the two you added, ask: **How do the people you know go about satisfying these needs? For example, do you see some kids trying to satisfy the need for importance by putting down others? Or do some kids drink at parties to be accepted?**

If possible, tell kids one way in which you've given in to temptation to satisfy a need. **Has something like that ever happened to you?**

If kids have trouble giving personal answers, have them discuss one or two hypothetical cases like these:

1. A girl's parents are divorced. She doesn't feel loved by either parent. She starts searching for love by "going all the way" with guys.

2. A guy comes to church regularly and says all the "right" words. But he does drugs during the rest of the week. He does all these things to be accepted—only by different groups of people.

What do you think is the best way to meet those same needs?

Listen to kids' answers. Then add comments like these:

There are two main ways to meet our needs. One is to "look out for number one" and try to meet them ourselves in ways that we understand and think are best. The other is to let God meet our needs in ways that He has provided.

Write the following words on the chalkboard or newsprint: Selfish, selfless, short-sighted, satisfying, sinful, sanctifying. Explain that sanctifying means to make pure or holy.

First, our way. Which of the words on this list describe the choices we tend to make when we try to satisfy our needs and desires our way? What does each of the words mean? (Likely possibilities: Selfish, just considering ourselves; short-sighted, not taking into account the lasting effects, usually one of which is harmful habits; and sinful, that which moves us away from God.) If kids choose other words, ask them to explain.

Have a volunteer read Jeremiah 17:5. **What tends to happen when we depend too much on ourselves?** (Our hearts turn away from the Lord.)

Being tempted to do the wrong thing isn't a sin. Giving in to that temptation is. But God made us with all of our needs and basic desires, and He knows they're good. After all, He put them there.

How about God's way of meeting our needs? Which words from the list apply? (Selfless, considerate of and helpful to others; satisfying, that which truly meets our needs for the long run; and sanctifying, that which helps us grow spiritually stronger and closer to God.) If kids choose other words, ask them to explain.

Have a volunteer read Jeremiah 17:7. **What do you need to believe about God in order to trust Him to meet your needs?** (That He really can meet your needs; you must have confidence in Him.)

Is that ever hard to do? Why? (Yes. He's invisible; we may fear that He doesn't care about us, that His plans for us differ from ours, etc.)

What's one need you find it hard to trust God to meet? Let kids think about this if they don't want to answer aloud. If possible, share an answer of your own.

Lion on the Loose
Spotting Satan's Strategy of Temptation

As you work on making the right choices, there's someone who's working against you. Have a group member read I Peter 5:8, 9.

Why do you think Peter compares the devil to a lion and says the lion is out to devour you? (Possibilities: The Romans threw Christians to the lions; the devil often "sneaks up" when he tempts us; he may frighten us with his strength, but it's possible to resist him.)

Peter makes it clear that you've got an enemy, the devil, who is out to make life very hard for you. He wants to make you feel like a failure. So when you give in to a temptation, he wants you to feel like the whole thing is hopeless and you might as well sin all you want, because that's the only way you'll ever feel good.

But that's a lie. It's Satan's strategy to get you to sin. He takes one of your needs or desires and tries to twist it toward sin by tempting you to meet it yourself.

How might the devil try to convince people that they have to meet their own needs in their own ways? (By convincing them that God isn't interested in their needs, or that He can't meet them; by offering substitutes that seem to meet needs, etc.)

According to the I Peter passage, what is our response to the devil supposed to be? (Resist him.)

What instructions in these verses could help us resist? (Be self-controlled and alert; stand firm in the faith; remember that other believers throughout the world face challenges from the devil, too.)

Ask a student to read I John 4:4. **Who is "the one who is in you"?** (Christ or the Holy Spirit, if you are a Christian.)

If the devil is like a lion, how would you describe "the one who is in you"? (Examples: A stronger lion; a lion tamer; a lion hunter.)

The devil is working against you, but you don't have to panic. He can offer you bad ideas, but he can't force you to choose them. God, who is in each person who belongs to Him, is infinitely more powerful than the devil.

Soak It to Me
Evaluating Our Resistance to Temptation

Before the session, fill an empty milk carton with water. Now hold up the carton. **What's this carton made of?** (Paper or cardboard.)

Hold up a lightweight paper bag. **What's this bag made of?** (Paper.)

Using a large pan to catch spills, pour a cup or two of water into the paper bag. Pretty soon the bag will start to leak and water will soak through.

Hey! The carton and the bag are basically made of the same thing. How come the bag doesn't hold the water like the carton does? (The carton is coated with plastic or wax.)

Point out that the carton *resists*—stands up against—moisture. The bag doesn't; it just soaks up—surrenders to—any liquid it touches.

When it comes to resisting temptation, are you more like a milk carton or a paper bag? Let kids think about this; they don't have to answer aloud.

If you resist a temptation the first time you encounter it, it's easier to resist the next time. If you keep resisting, it keeps getting easier. The opposite is true, too. Give in the first time, and it's harder to resist next time. Keep

giving in, and it's harder and harder to resist. Before you know it you've built a habit.

Even when you keep trying to "do the right thing," you slip up once in a while. It's sin, but God offers forgiveness. So when you fall into sin, you can get back up, confess your sin, and keep pressing on.

Close with silent prayer, giving kids a chance to tell God about needs they may have been trying to meet in their own way, or sins they want to confess. If you plan to use other sessions in this unit, let kids know you'll be talking in more detail about handling temptation.

Only God can meet our deepest needs, and He meets them through Jesus Christ. But exactly how does that work? If kids don't know, they'll have a hard time trusting God to meet their needs. And that means they'll be more likely to give in to tempting substitutes that only *seem* to meet their needs.

In this session, you'll help group members see that God can and will meet their needs—and how to start letting God do that in the specific areas in which they're tempted.

God Has a Better Idea

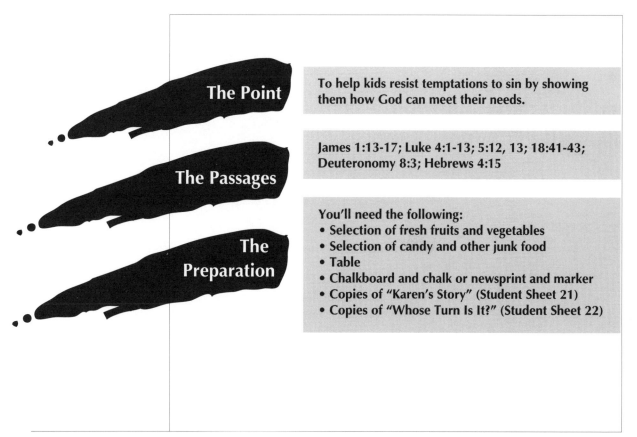

The Point	To help kids resist temptations to sin by showing them how God can meet their needs.
The Passages	James 1:13-17; Luke 4:1-13; 5:12, 13; 18:41-43; Deuteronomy 8:3; Hebrews 4:15
The Preparation	You'll need the following: • Selection of fresh fruits and vegetables • Selection of candy and other junk food • Table • Chalkboard and chalk or newsprint and marker • Copies of "Karen's Story" (Student Sheet 21) • Copies of "Whose Turn Is It?" (Student Sheet 22)

A Fruitful Lesson
Learning the Difference between Wants and Needs

Bring a selection of fresh fruits and vegetables and a selection of candy and other "junk" food. Set these out on a table. Either (1) invite kids to help themselves as they arrive, or (2) don't let them choose until the meeting starts. If the group is very large, you may want to limit the diners to several volunteers. In any case, it's likely that more junk food than health food will be picked up.

When given a choice of what to eat, we often pick sweets and snack foods over fruits and vegetables. Why do you think that is? (Junk food doesn't have to be peeled or cooked, it's usually sweeter or saltier, its flavor is stronger, it's packaged to entice us, we associate it with good times, etc.)

When it comes to food, we have real needs and we have wants. What are some of our real food needs? (We need enough protein, vitamins, minerals, carbohydrates, water, etc. to live.)

What are some of our "food wants"? (The "up" feeling we get from sugar or caffiene; food that smells and looks inviting; textures [like chewiness or carbonation] that feel good in our mouths; food that's quick and easy to prepare and eat, etc.)

Which meets more of our real needs—fruits and vegetables or junk food? (Fruits and vegetables.)

Which do you think meets more of our real needs—doing things our way or God's way? Some kids will automatically say, "God's way." Encourage them to give an example. Others may question whether God really meets people's needs at all. Let them know that you'll give an example of God's need-meeting in the next step.

Karen's Story
Seeing How God Met One Person's Real Needs

Speaking of food, here's the true story of a person who was tempted to eat—too much. Pass out copies of "Karen's Story" (Student Sheet 21). Read it together or have kids read it on their own. Then discuss, using questions like these:

What were Karen's real, deep-down needs? (Acceptance, friends, love.)

How did she try to meet these needs on her own? (By becoming a class clown and by trying to comfort herself with food.)

Why did she have such a hard time with temptation? (She got caught in a cycle—the more she gave in to temptation the worse she felt, which made it even harder to resist the next temptation.)

How did God meet her real needs? (By accepting and loving her no matter how much she weighed, and by helping her to develop self-control. Even more important, He gave her eternal life.)

If God is meeting her needs, why is Karen still tempted sometimes? (She's not perfect yet, and habits are hard to break. But she makes progress with God's help.)

Can you name a need that God has met for you or for someone you know? Be ready to share an example from your own life, too.

Step 3

What We're Up Against
Seeing How Satan Uses Desire to Tempt Us

Have a volunteer read James 1:13-17.

What do these verses tell you about temptation? (God doesn't tempt us, and He isn't tempted; we're tempted because of our own wrong desires; first comes the desire, then the sin, then the penalty.)

What could verses 16 and 17 have to do with temptation? (A possibility: Every good thing comes from God; it never comes from the tempter, who offers substitutes.)

What are some examples of "evil desires"? What are some things people want but shouldn't have? (Revenge; other people's possessions; to have power over others; to have sex with anyone they find attractive, etc.)

What are some good desires God has created in us? (The will to survive, to have families, to eat and drink, to know God, etc.)

If you have time, provide a biblical example of a good desire. Have a student read Luke 18:41-43.

This man had a desire to see. Jesus fulfilled the man's desire. Notice the two times "want" appears. What does this story tell you about Jesus? (A possibility: that He cares about people's real needs and wants to meet them.)

Jesus Himself was tempted. Let's look at Luke 4:1-13 to see what we can find about how God can meet our needs and help us resist temptation.

Have one or more group members read the passage about the temptation of Jesus in the wilderness.

What need was Satan using in the first temptation? (The need for food or the need to survive.)

How did Jesus respond? (He quoted a passage from the Old Testament [see Deuteronomy 8:3].)

Jesus was starving after 40 days without food. Why did He talk about living on God's words instead of bread alone? What was Jesus saying about the way His need would be met? (He was saying that God would take care of Him. He depended on God, who makes all food, to live.)

Look at the second temptation from Satan. What need does it aim at? (The need for importance or recognition.)

Jesus had these needs, too. Hebrews 4:15 assures us, "We have one [Jesus] who has been tempted in every way, just as we are—yet was without sin." But Jesus realized that His relationship with the Father gave him all the importance He needed.

Then the third temptation from Satan attacked this relationship. Did the Father *really* love Jesus? If He did, He wouldn't let Jesus get hurt. Recognize that need? (The need for love and acceptance.)

Jesus replied that no one should test God. But then He didn't need to. He had confidence in God's ability to take care of Him.

God wants to meet your needs, too.

Have a volunteer read Matthew 6:31-34.

What does this tell you about God and your needs? (He already sees our needs and wants to meet them; He doesn't want us to worry about them; He wants us to put Him first and trust Him to provide for us.)

Declaration of Dependence
Learning How to Trust God to Meet Our Needs

Distribute copies of "Be Prepared" (Student Sheet 22). Look over the sheet with students, discussing the three suggestions. As needed, add questions and comments like the following:

1. Now you may be asking, "Wait on God? Does that mean I pray and then wait around for God to send me a typed, double-spaced term paper next time I get assigned one?"

What do you think is the answer? Listen to kids' replies.

Someone has said, "God is responsible to meet your needs. You need to meet your responsibilities." What do you think that means? (God does His part, and we do ours.)

Use the following example if you like: Steve needs friends. God cares and wants to provide companionship for Steve. But it's Steve's responsibility to be friendly to others in order to make friends. If the only friends Steve can find are kids who pressure him to do drugs, he needs to back off and wait for God to help him find other friends. But Steve has to keep looking and being friendly.

2. What other ways can you think of to get to know God better? (Asking older Christians what they've learned about God; looking at His creation for clues about what He's like; read biographies of people who have trusted Him before, etc.)

3. How do we usually want God to meet our needs? (Right away, in the way that's most convenient for us.) **Why might God take a while to meet a person's need?** (So the person will learn to trust God, or to not take Him for granted; to meet another person's need at the same time; to draw the person closer to Him or teach the person to put God's priorities first; or sometimes for reasons we won't know until we get to heaven.)

Teaming Up on Temptation
Using Accountability to Help Us Resist Temptation

If kids in your group are used to being open with each other, have them get together in pairs (preferably of the same sex). Ask them to share with each other one temptation they faced last week and how they handled it.

Close with group prayer, or prayer in pairs. Encourage kids to commit their needs to God, and ask Him to help them take the three steps you just talked about:

• Trust God to meet your needs.
• Get closer to God.
• Let God meet your needs in the way He knows is best.

When kids—or adults—work on something and don't see results quickly, they can get frustrated. Whether or not you've worked through other sessions in this unit, you may find some kids discouraged about the topic of temptation when they arrive.

That can be a good sign. Those who are most frustrated over temptation may be those who are trying to resist it.

This session focuses on one important reason why temptation gets the better of us even when we seem to know the spiritual facts of life. You'll encourage kids to go beyond knowing the facts—to believing them.

A Losing Battle?

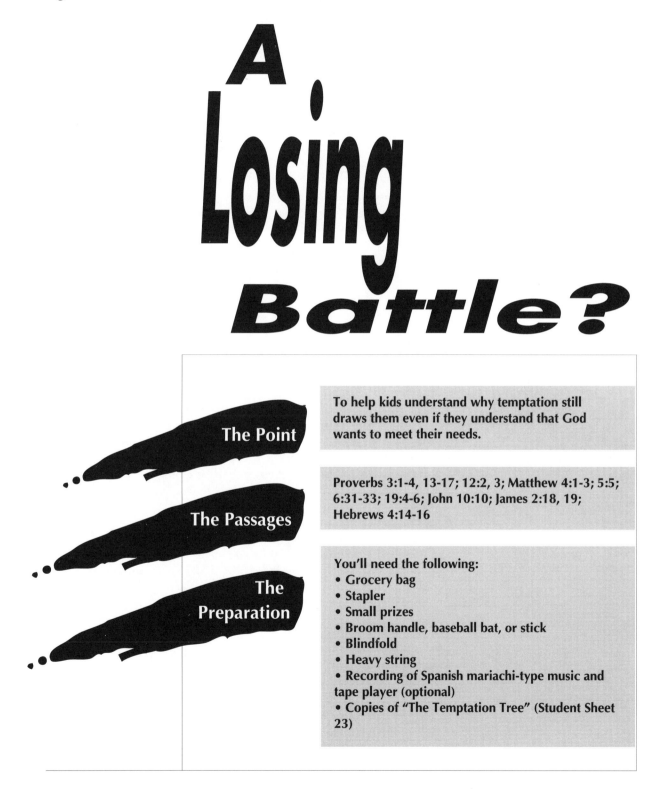

The Point

To help kids understand why temptation still draws them even if they understand that God wants to meet their needs.

The Passages

Proverbs 3:1-4, 13-17; 12:2, 3; Matthew 4:1-3; 5:5; 6:31-33; 19:4-6; John 10:10; James 2:18, 19; Hebrews 4:14-16

The Preparation

You'll need the following:
• Grocery bag
• Stapler
• Small prizes
• Broom handle, baseball bat, or stick
• Blindfold
• Heavy string
• Recording of Spanish mariachi-type music and tape player (optional)
• Copies of "The Temptation Tree" (Student Sheet 23)

The Big Bag Bash
Seeing the Frustration of Fighting Temptation on Our Own

Before the meeting, put together a very simple piñata. Fill a grocery bag with small prizes (candy, cheap toys, an old book, etc.) and staple it shut. Make sure the prizes won't get broken when kids bash the bag. If you want to get fancy, decorate the bag with paint or markers.

Also bring a stick-like object (baseball bat, broom, etc.) and a scarf or bandanna to use as a blindfold. For atmosphere, you might plan to play Spanish or Mexican music during the piñata-bashing.

At the meeting, hang the bag from a tree branch or sturdy ceiling hook. Line kids up to take turns bashing the piñata. One at a time, blindfolded, students should be spun around and allowed to take three swings each. When the bag breaks open, let kids scramble for the prizes.

After things settle down, ask: **How does it feel to try to hit a target you can't see?** (Probably frustrating.)

Dealing with temptation can prove just as frustrating as trying to hit a target while blindfolded. What do you find frustrating about temptation? Be ready to share an answer of your own. Possibilities include the fact that we can be tempted over and over by the same things; we can resist one day but give in the next; we may feel trapped by habits, etc.

We may know all sorts of facts about how temptation works on us. But we can still be frustrated when we try to stand up to it. God wants to help us take off our "blindfolds" and fight temptation more effectively.

Believing Is Seeing
Understanding That What We Believe Affects What We Do

Ask kids what they think this statement means: "We do what we believe."

After listening to answers, comment along these lines:

What we believe about anything—cars, people, happiness, whatever—strongly affects what we do. If you believe the world is flat, you won't go sailing far from shore. If you believe you're great at basketball, you'll go out for the team and give it your best. If you believe sex gets you love, you'll go all the way. Can you think of other examples of how a belief could affect your actions?

After kids have offered suggestions, continue: **Let's take a closer look at this, and see how it relates to temptation.**

We have beliefs about a lot of things. One of them is how we can meet our most basic needs—like our needs for love, acceptance, and importance.

Hand out Student Sheet 23, "The Temptation Tree." Call attention to the diagram. Read the steps, working your way up from "Need" to "Habit." **See how it works?**

Use this example if you'd like, working your way up the tree.

Need: Tami needs love and acceptance.

Belief: She believes that God's acceptance of her is not enough, and that her mother can satisfy her need.

Attitude: She wants her mother to show her respect, but her mother can't or won't do that in a way Tami can see.

Action: Tami gets angry at her mother because she doesn't feel re-spected. Arguing seems to at least get her mother's attention.

Habit: Tami can't seem to talk with her mother for more than five minutes without a fight breaking out.

How could a change in belief help Tami? (She needs to believe that God's acceptance of her is enough—that only God's love and acceptance can meet her need, in fact.)

Tami can't change her need for love and acceptance. How could she start to change her belief? (Talk to a mature Christian about the way she sees herself and sees God; find out about God's promises in the Bible; talk to someone who's had a similar problem; read about how God has helped others in the past, etc.)

Once her belief changes, how could that change her attitudes and actions? As needed, supplement kids' answers by explaining that when Tami really believes God can and will meet her need, she'll develop a new attitude toward God. She can ask Him to meet this need, and wait on Him to do it. She'll value herself more because she'll believe God created her specifically and loves her completely. When she doesn't tie her value to what her mother says and does, she'll probably be more patient and understanding toward her mother.

Don't get the wrong idea. It will still hurt when Tami's mother doesn't treat her the way she wants to be treated. She'll still have to work on turning away from her old belief. But now she'll know which way to head. She'll know the right belief she can turn to when she's tempted to get into a fight with her mom.

So, to review: How does a bad habit form? (You try to meet a need or basic desire on your own one time, and it feels good even though it's a sin. So you believe this is a way to meet that need. You keep doing it, and you form a habit.)

Someone to Believe In
Correcting Wrong Beliefs with Biblical Truth

Pass out copies of "Don't You Believe It!" (Student Sheet 24). Have students, working individually or in small groups, come up with biblical "corrections" for the mistaken beliefs listed on the sheet. Then discuss the results, using the following information as needed:

1. Correction (Proverbs 3:1-4): Knowing and obeying God's commands doesn't make you a reject—when you keep the big picture in mind. Obeying pleases God, and in the long run, gives you a "good name" with others.

2. Correction (Matthew 4:1-3; Hebrews 4:14-16): Jesus (God the Son) went hungry for 40 days in the desert. He understands our weaknesses, having been tempted as we are.

3. Correction (Matthew 19:4-6): God created sex. His plan is for husband and wife to find a special oneness through their relationship, an important part of which is sexual. God's attitude toward sex is positive, and following His commands make sexuality constructive instead of destructive.

4. Correction (Matthew 5:5): Getting revenge seems satisfying for a while, but God promises great rewards and long-range justice to those who leave "getting even" to Him. We can work to see that people are treated fairly, but not at the expense of forgiving enemies or letting God be the ultimate Judge.

5. Correction (Proverbs 12:2, 3; Matthew 6:31-33): A dishonest foundation is a shaky one, and in the long run God will make sure it crumbles. He's promised that doing things His way will lead to our having all we need

(though not necessarily all we want).

6. Correction (Proverbs 3:13-17; John 10:10): Nothing we desire can compare with the benefit we get from following God's way. Jesus came to give us life "to the full," a life of joy instead of misery.

If time allows, read or paraphrase the following case studies to help kids apply the biblical principles.

1. Jay needs love and acceptance. When he was seven, his parents divorced. His father left, making Jay feel abandoned, angry, and unwanted. Jay began to believe that no one close to him could accept him. He learned an attitude of holding people at a distance and not trusting adults. Now he's using drugs. They seem to help him forget about his feelings—at least while he's high. What right beliefs should replace Jay's mistaken one?

(Possibilities: That no one can accept him, because God can; that no one can be trusted, because God can; and that numbing his bad feelings is better than dealing with their cause.)

2. Kathleen is the second of three kids, stuck in the middle, over-looked—never old enough to do anything or young enough to get away with anything. She has come to believe that she isn't important just by herself, that she needs something more. Now she's dating an older guy as a status symbol. To keep him, she's in the habit of having sex with him. She thinks that isn't a bad trade-off for her new status. What right beliefs should replace Kathleen's mistaken ones?

(Possibilities: That she's not important, because God says she is; that status symbols can make her important; that status is more important than obeying God.)

Climbing the Tree
Helping Students Identify Wrong Beliefs That Hinder Them

So much about Tami and Jay and Kathleen. What about you? Are wrong beliefs keeping you from letting God meet your needs His way?

Ask kids to bow their heads and complete these statements silently. Pause after each.

I've got this bad habit. It bothers me that I keep . . .

I think my real need in this area might be . . .

When it comes to God meeting my need, I've believed . . .

But the best way to meet my need is . . .

Note: At best, kids have reached mental agreement that a certain belief is right. But taking action is something else.

Read James 2:18, 19. **James is saying that mental agreement isn't what counts, but action based on that knowledge and faith. True belief results in action and a changed life.**

You always choose how to respond to a temptation. A strong belief about how to meet a need through sin can make it harder to choose, but nothing ever takes away your power to choose. You're the one who decides what to believe, and what to do about it.

If possible, offer to talk later with kids who are struggling with specific temptations. Close in prayer.

In the battle to overcome temptation, it helps to have a clear conscience. No one has a perfectly clean track record, but running the spiritual race is harder than ever when you're hampered by sin and guilt.

Kids need to know the benefit of cleaning up their pasts and keeping the present clean, too. In this session, they'll learn how to take an important step in battling temptation: conquering inner space, the heart and mind.

Clearing Up Your Conscience

The Point

To help kids see the benefits of battling temptation, confessing sin, and receiving God's forgiveness when they fall.

The Passages

Acts 20:24; I Corinthians 9:24; Galatians 5:7; II Timothy 4:7; Hebrews 12:1; Matthew 5:21, 22; Luke 5:31; Psalm 32:5; I John 1:9; Romans 10:9

The Preparation

You'll need the following:
• Two heavy overcoats, two pairs of large boots, two paper plates, two marbles (optional)
• Overcoat with weights, stopwatch (optional)
• Two pairs of mittens (optional)
• Small prizes (optional)
• Bibles
• Pencils
• Copies of "Who's to Blame?" (Student Sheet 25)
• Copies of "Clearing the Air" (Student Sheet 26)

Winded Sprints
Seeing How Weights and Entanglements Slow Us Down

Try starting the session with an activity that shows how weights and entanglements slow a person down. Depending on your setting, choose one or more of the following:

1. *Ridiculous Relay.* Form two teams. The first runner on each team must put on a heavy overcoat and large boots you've brought. Then he or she must carry a marble in a paper plate to a line you've established—without dropping the marble—and return to the starting point. If the marble is dropped, that person must start his or her turn over.

The first runner then passes the coat, boots, pan, and marble to the next runner in line, and the race continues.

2. *Poundage Parka.* Before the session, put large stones or other weights in the pockets of an overcoat. Try to make the coat at least ten pounds heavier than normal.

Ask a volunteer to try out a new fitness training device you've thought up. Tell kids they may have heard about Heavy Hands, but this is the "Poundage Parka" for total body training.

Have the volunteer run a short distance without the coat to set a benchmark time. Then have him or her put on the jacket and time the run again. Compare the times and the runner's comments.

3. *Fumbling Finders.* If you don't have room for running, try a "sword drill" in which kids race to see who can first look up a Bible reference (or hymn number) you call out. But have the competitors wear mittens as they try to look up the verses or hymns. Unless you have lots of mittens, you may want to limit the competitors to two and have the rest of the kids cheer them on.

Whichever activity you choose, award prizes if you wish. Then discuss the activity with questions like these:

What effect did the (coats, boots, weights, or mittens) have?

How would you dress if you wanted to do your best at this activity?

What would you think of a person who claimed to be a runner but slowed himself or herself down during a race with extra weight and the wrong clothes? (Probably that he or she was strange, phony, inexperienced, or didn't care about winning.)

The Race Is On
Running the Christian Race without the Weight of Sin

Have you ever heard the Christian life compared to a race?

Get volunteers to read these verses: Acts 20:24; I Corinthians 9:24; Galatians 5:7; II Timothy 4:7.

How is the Christian life like a race? (There's a task to be completed, a limited amount of time to do it in, a reward offered, the possibility of interference with your ability to run, etc.)

What's the goal of this race? (A possible answer: To stay on course, serving God faithfully.)

When you first learn to run, you don't start out running a marathon. You may not even make it around the block without falling down. As you run, you get stronger and faster. You may also lose weight. In running the spiritual race, you're supposed to lose a different kind of weight.

Read Hebrews 12:1.

What are some of the things that "hinder" people in the Christian life?
(Wanting money more than we want to know God; devoting too much time to less important things like entertainment; sinful habits; guilt; not knowing what we believe, etc.)

One thing that entangles us is sin. It's like tying your legs together with a steel chain, wrapping it around and around. Try running with that on!

All this has something to do with temptation. To handle temptation, we need to "throw off everything that hinders and the sin that so easily entangles." That means unloading your mind, conscience, and spirit of the extra baggage of sin.

Nobody Made You Do It
Admitting Responsibility for Our Actions

How do you dump the weight of sin from your life?
Listen to kids' responses. Explain that the first step is seeing who is really responsible for our sins.

Distribute copies of "Who's to Blame?" (Student Sheet 25) and have each student complete the exercise. Discuss the results. Explain that the answer to each question is 100 %. Each person (Pat, Janine, the sarcastic girl, Teresa, Debi, Anthony, and each of the kids involved in the murder) is responsible for his or her response to temptation.

One of the dangers in temptation is the tendency to blame others for part or all of the results. But every sin I've ever committed is completely my responsibility.

Think about that for a second. What about a girl whose mother, a crack addict, sells her to the mother's dealer to pay off a drug debt? If the girl wants to kill her mother, is that a sin? What if she just hates her mother?

It would be easier to tell you no, to tell you that in those cases the sin would be the fault of the other person. But the Bible teaches that any wrong response is a sin.
Read Matthew 5:21, 22 as an example.
Does that seem fair to you?
Allow kids to discuss this honestly. If they feel that some provocations are just too much—that some people deserve to be hated, stolen from, or even murdered—you may want to remind them that God forgives us through Christ even though we don't deserve it.

To get free from a temptation, you must acknowledge your sin in giving into the temptation. Completely. It's not 75% your fault, or even 95%. It's 100%. If other people are involved, they are 100% responsible for any sin on their part. But you—and only you—are responsible for your response to temptation.

Cleaning Your Slate
Leading Students to Confession and Forgiveness

Admitting and accepting full responsibility for our sinful responses is the first step in getting rid of the things that weigh us down. The second step is to confess wrongdoing to one another and make necessary restitution (restoring something) to people we've hurt. Then we've won a major battle against temptation.

Hand out Student Sheet 26, "Clearing the Air." Discuss as a group the actions a person should take if he or she had committed these sins. As needed, share these suggestions:

Robbing a bank. This should be confessed to God and the police, and perhaps to others who would be hurt by the robbery. The money should be returned. Honest work should replace robbery as a way of making a living.

Thinking lustful thoughts. This should be confessed to God. If the thoughts become a hard-to-break habit, it would be good to confess to and discuss the matter with a counselor or other mature Christian adult. Restitution may not apply in this case. Thinking more about unselfish love, finding out what the Bible says about sex, and forming healthy, nonsexual friendships could gradually crowd out many of these thoughts.

Making fun of a friend behind her back. This should be confessed to God, to the friend who was hurt, and to those who may think less of the friend because of the ridicule. This confession, along with working to regain the friend's trust, would be restitution. Making fun of the friend could be replaced with accepting the friend as she is.

As you ask God to show you sins to confess, the Holy Spirit will show you things that are specific and that can be dealt with. God doesn't make you feel hopeless or forever guilty about anything.

Knowing that, don't worry if God shows you a lot of specific, even small things you have to dump. Jesus said, "It is not the healthy who need a doctor, but the sick. I have not come to call the righteous, but sinners to repentance" (Luke 5:31).

If time allows, ask kids to look at Student Sheet 26 again, thinking about their own lives. Give them an opportunity to pray silently, asking God to remind them of sins they need to accept responsibility for, confess, ask forgiveness for, or make restitution for. Be sure to explain, though, that making restitution is not a way of *earning* favor with God; it's a matter of obedience and restoring relationships. God's forgiveness through Christ is a free gift.

A Forgiving Father
Seeing the Freedom in God's Forgiveness

Confessing is pretty serious work. Thinking about your sins can make you feel weighed down—instead of feeling ready to run a race. But forgiveness really does lead to freedom. Here are a couple of things to remember:

1. As you take any action you need to outside this meeting on these sins, you will start feeling free.

2. Remember that God has completely forgiven you of all the guilt of your sin now that you have confessed it.

Have volunteers read Psalm 32:5 and I John 1:9.

If possible, share with kids an example of how confession and forgiveness have worked in your life. How have they helped you feel free and ready to run the race again?

We usually think of confessing as something negative, admitting the sin we've committed. But there's a good side to the word, too. The apostle Paul wrote, "That if you *confess* with your mouth, 'Jesus is Lord,' and believe in your heart that God raised him from the dead, you will be saved (Romans 10:9).

If time allows, put kids in pairs. Each partner should confess to the other either (1) a wrong response he or she has made to temptation, or (2) a positive statement about God's power to completely forgive.

Close in prayer, thanking God for His freeing gift of forgiveness.

Like the rest of us, most teenagers have a hard time staying focused on a goal, no matter how worthy it is. In this session, you'll help kids understand how to keep moving toward the right goal—even if they momentarily forget what the goal is! And you'll help them prepare for the long road ahead of battling— and beating—temptation for the rest of their lives.

Feeling Stronger Every Day

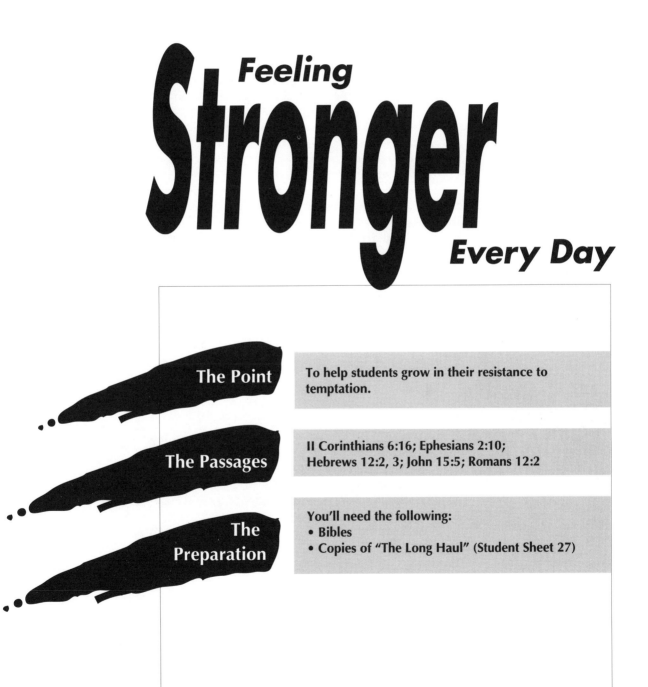

The Point	To help students grow in their resistance to temptation.
The Passages	II Corinthians 6:16; Ephesians 2:10; Hebrews 12:2, 3; John 15:5; Romans 12:2
The Preparation	You'll need the following: • Bibles • Copies of "The Long Haul" (Student Sheet 27)

Surprise!

Admitting a Lack of Urgency about Resisting Temptation

If you choose to open your meeting with this scenario, try to "get into the mood" before you do. You'll want to come across as if you're bursting with big news. But don't overdo it, or kids will see straight through your scheme.

I don't know quite how to tell you this. Maybe you've heard of those books that have come out saying that the second coming of Jesus will happen at a specific time. Well, another came out a few months ago—predicting that two weeks from today, Jesus will return. I looked it over yesterday, and it actually made sense! The chances are good that it's true! We've got just two weeks to get ready!

Pause for about five seconds.

What just went through your mind?

Field some answers.

Some of you probably thought I was crazy. Or maybe you felt pumped up, excited. Others may have started making a mental checklist of sins to confess when you got home tonight, albums to throw away, things to give back to other people. Or maybe you were a little scared.

I made up the stuff about the book. But if you *did* somehow find out that Jesus would return in two weeks, what would change in your life?

Field some responses.

How would it change the way you deal with temptation? (We might be more likely to resist temptation, knowing that we wouldn't have to fight it much longer. We might also resist because we'd soon be facing the Lord.)

We should probably deal with temptation every day as if we had no more than two weeks. Why don't we? (We get tired; we don't see results; we let other things become more important to us than Jesus is, etc.)

Keeping our eyes on Jesus—no matter when He returns—can help us deal with temptation every day. Let's find out how.

Under Construction

Taking a Long-range View of Our Struggles with Temptation

Tell this story:

A man walked past a crew of three construction workers. He stopped and asked them, "What are you doing?"

The first answered, "Putting bricks together."

The second said, "Building a wall."

The third replied, "Constructing a cathedral," and he pointed at the sky where the spires would reach.

Which of these workers do you think would get tired of his job first? (Probably the one who thought he was just putting bricks together. The one who kept the goal—a cathedral—in mind might be more motivated to keep going until the job was finished.)

When you stand up to temptations, one at a time, you're not just putting bricks together. It all adds up to something really important.

Have volunteers read II Corinthians 6:16 and Ephesians 2:10. Ask: **What building project are we compared to?** (The temple of the living God).

Who is constructing the building? (God is.)

If you belong to Christ, it's as if you're becoming part of a magnificent cathedral in honor of God. He's doing the work in you. You can't do it by

yourself. God already has the blueprints for the cathedral, and He's building it brick by brick.

When you stand up to temptation, you're also building walls of resistance to future temptation. But ultimately you're becoming the beautiful temple of God.

Your part is to cooperate with Him—one step at a time. Keep in mind the ultimate goal, but realize that it happens one step at a time. You just need to know which brick to pick up next.

Keeping On Keeping On
Understanding Our Need to Focus on Jesus

Step 3

Let's say you go to a Christian camp. While you're there a speaker talks about getting right with God, and really gets to you. You've been having trouble with certain sins for a long time, and now you want more than ever to please God. You promise Him that this time when you get home from camp, things will be different. For a couple of weeks they are. **What happens next?** (Answers will vary, but it's common for a "mountaintop experience" like this to fade—and for old habits to creep back.)

Getting all fired up can keep us focused on a goal for awhile. But longer-term goals are another matter. We get a few days or weeks away from a commitment and our memory starts to fade. We start to get comfortable. We settle into a routine. We look around and see what other people are doing and what they have.

We can lose our motivation to work on a goal, no matter how hard we try. One business expert has said that if you don't start working on a goal within 72 hours after setting it, you'll never achieve it.

So in our battle against temptation, how do we stay motivated? How can we keep from getting discouraged and slipping back into the problem we had before?

Listen to kids' suggestions. Then have a volunteer read Hebrews 12:2, 3.

What's the advice here? (Fix your eyes on Jesus, who kept going despite all kinds of opposition.)

How can you fix (keep) your eyes on Jesus? (Think about Him, talk with Him, read about Him, follow His example, etc.)

Jesus knows the way to the goal. In fact, He *is* the way. Have volunteers read John 14:6 and John 15:5.

What do you think it means to remain in Christ? (To rely on Him, stick with Him, keep learning from Him, etc. The whole idea is to stay close to Christ for the rest of your life.)

The point of all this is two-part:

1. You have to depend on Jesus to help you keep beating temptation.

2. You need to take it one step at a time.

Does that make you feel worse or better about temptation? (Opinions will vary. But when we see that we aren't alone and that we can take things a step at a time, it takes some of the pressure off.)

Brain Change
Finding Ways to Renew Our Minds

Form three groups. Each group is to look up and paraphrase Romans 12:2 as follows: Group 1, in words that a third grader would understand; Group 2, in words a scientist or computer expert might use; and Group 3, as a poem or rap. Be ready to help the groups if they have trouble understanding some phrases in the original verse.

Regather the whole group and share results, which might sound something like this:

Group 1: "If you just think and act the way most people do, you'll end up doing some very wrong things. Instead, learn to see things the way God does by learning all you can about Him. Then you'll know when to do what others do—and when to be different."

Group 2: "Do not let a computer virus into your system; it could scramble your data. Instead, erase faulty programs from your disk and replace them with ones that are free of bugs, so that your computations are accurate."

Group 3: "You need to change, but not to fit the other guys, no, not a bit; just let the true things change your mind, and then the truth you'll surely find."

How could you put this verse into practice?

Listen to reponses. To supplement them, pass out copies of Student Sheet 27, "The Long Haul." If you have time, read the sheet together. Then have kids pair up to discuss how they could put the "accountability friends" idea into practice.

Encourage kids to form and maintain accountability relationships. Be ready to bring the subject up at the next meeting; you may want to ask kids to sign up then to be in pairs for a "trial run" of one to three months.

If possible, offer to work with kids outside the meeting time if they're struggling with temptation. Then close in prayer.

Do the Right Thing?

How would you feel in these situations?

1. Everyone's at the party—at least everyone you like. You're playing it safe, avoiding the drinking. Then your friend offers you a beer—just as that cute new person of the opposite sex walks past.

　　You don't want that person to think you're a geek, so you take the drink. It doesn't taste too bad. You have another.

　　The next day your head hurts a little. But, man, last night you had the best time with your friends that you've ever had! Or at least that's the way you remember it.

2. Your boss at the clothing store *always* asks you to work an hour more than you're supposed to. And then he won't pay you for overtime!

　　After a while you figure the company owes you more than $200. So you take home a $30 sweater that you've been wanting. You know you'll get away with it, because your boss trusts you. Besides, you think, they've been using you just because you're a teenager. And the sweater does look good on you.

3. After eight months of dating, your steady dumps you like a load of used football practice jerseys. You're so mad and hurt you can't see straight.

　　So when you're talking with a friend the next day, you hint that your former steady is secretly afraid of the dark. Later that day, you hear people passing on the rumor and laughing about it.

You Need What?

Write next to each whether it's a need, a want, or a like.

New car_____
School hot lunch _____
Friends_____
CD player _____
Bed _____
After-school job _____
Water _____

College _____
New jeans _____
Athletic ability _____
School bus ride _____
Place to live _____
Tennis lessons _____
Girlfriend or boyfriend _____
Computer _____

Karen's Story

I didn't want to be weird and different. I wanted someone to choose me out of the crowd and say, "You are my special friend. I like you because you're you."

But it didn't take me long to realize life was not going to treat me that kindly. By the time I entered junior high, I had reached some painful conclusions about myself: I would always be fat, I would never be beautiful, and I would never have dates like other girls.

As far as I was concerned, I had two choices: I could shrink back into the shadows and disappear among the wallflowers, or I could turn myself into a three-ring circus and laugh my troubles away. I chose the circus, and no one ever forgot my performances.

• • • • • • • • • • • • • • • • • • •

In public I laughed. In private I ate. Food became my comforter for the rejection I felt. . . . I eventually ate my way to 340 pounds.

I occasionally attempted to break the cycle. I would determine to stop over-eating . . . but most of my efforts ended in disaster.

• • • • • • • • • • • • • • • • • • •

I began to mistrust people. I was afraid and alone. . . . I built a high, hard wall around myself for protection and thought nothing could penetrate it. For years, nothing did.

But one day my defenses cracked. . . . A Christian friend of mine wrote a song that talked about God's love. That song penetrated me and described precisely what I needed. I began to see that God *did* accept me and cared about me even the way I was.

• • • • • • • • • • • • • • • • • • •

After I gave my life to Him I found He helped me do what, through all the years of struggle, I could never do for myself. After I became a Christian, God gave me a gift—self-control. It was not a magic prescription like a diet pill. . . . It was, rather, a slow, painful process: days and weeks and even years of saying "no" when I desperately wanted to say "yes."

Today I am 200 pounds lighter. Some days I feel like the new creation I am in Christ. Other days I think of myself as the same unlovable, unacceptable Karen, and I worry about what people think of me. But I guess that just goes to show that God and I still have some projects we need to work on.

• • • • • • • • • • • • • • • • • • •

—From "Weigh to Go" by Karen Wise with Ruth Senter, *The Campus Life Guide to Surviving High School*, ©1984 by Campus Life Books.

Be Prepared

Temptation's going to come your way. How can you get ready to face it? Here are three suggestions.

1 *Trust God to meet your needs.*

Don't just rely on yourself. Before you're faced with temptation, commit all your needs to God. Ask Him to meet your needs. Then whenever you're faced with a temptation, think through what it promises. It's probably a poor substitute for what God wants to do for you. Wait on Him to meet your real, deep-down needs.

2 *Develop your relationship with God.*

It's great to make the choice to trust God with your needs. But as time passes and you get farther away from that commitment, resisting temptation can get harder. To make it easier to trust God, get to know Him better.

Do this by spending time with Him. Many Christians throughout the centuries have found reading the Bible and praying to be two effective ways of knowing God better.

3 *Don't try to force God to meet your needs in the way you want.*

Let God show you through the Bible and His Holy Spirit how He can best meet your needs.

You might try scanning the Bible for ways in which God has already met a need like yours in the lives of others. You could also look for promises that tell how He will meet needs like yours.

The Temptation Tree

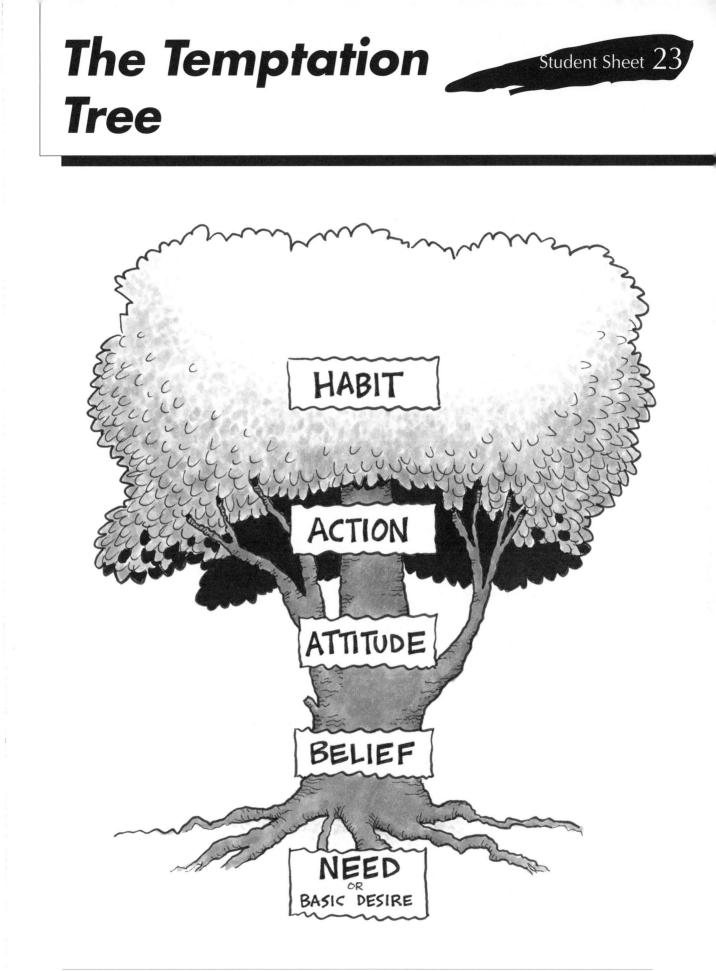

Don't You Believe It!

Here are six statements some people believe. Try correcting them, using the Scripture verses listed.

1. "Sure, it's a sleazy movie. But if I refuse to go, kids will think I'm a geek. I'll be a reject if they don't think I'm cool."
Correction (Proverbs 3:1-4):

2. "I really need to go on eating binges sometimes. God couldn't understand that—He doesn't have a physical body, so He doesn't know what it's like to be hungry."
Correction (Matthew 4:1-3; Hebrews 4:14-16):

3. "God may care about most of my needs, but sex is something else. He doesn't get involved in that except to say no."
Correction (Matthew 19:4-6):

4. "If somebody hurts me, I'll have to fight back. That's the only way to make sure people get what they deserve."
Correction (Matthew 5:5):

5. "If I don't cheat on this test, I won't pass the course. Then I won't graduate, and I'll never get a job and have enough money to live on."
Correction (Proverbs 12:2, 3; Matthew 6:31-33):

6. "This activity may be wrong, but it makes me feel good. If I stop doing everything the Bible says is wrong, I'll be miserable."
Correction (Proverbs 3:13-17; John 10:10):

Who's to Blame?

Who's responsible when a person gives in to a temptation and commits a sin? Society? Other people? The devil?

How much responsibility do you think each of the following people has for the way he or she responds to the temptation described? Mark a spot along each percentage line to show your answer.

1. *The Temptation:* Pat wants a pair of stereo headphones, but doesn't have the money for them. At the music store he finds a pair he really likes. Suddenly the clerk at the cash register locks up the cash drawer and goes into the back room to get a new roll of register tape.

The Response: While the clerk is in the back room, Pat slips the headphones under his coat and walks out of the store.

The Responsibility:

0% Pat's _____ 100% Pat's

2. *The Temptation:* Janine is walking down the hall between classes when she slips and falls. Her books tumble all over the floor. As she painfully picks herself up, she hears one of the more popular girls say sarcastically, "Hey, Graceful, have a nice trip?"

The Response: Janine snaps back, "The floor wouldn't be so slick if it weren't for slime like you."

The Responsibility:

0% Janine's _____ 100% Janine's

3. *The Temptation:* Teresa has been invited by her friend Debi to go to a party Friday night. Teresa knows her parents wouldn't want her to go, since there probably will be drinking and a lot of guy-girl fooling around. Debi knows this, too, so she asks Teresa's mom, "Can Teresa come to my house Friday night to study? We've got a big algebra test Monday."

The Response: Teresa says nothing, letting her mom think Debi's telling the truth.

The Responsibility:

0% Teresa's _____ 100% Teresa's

4. *The Temptation:* Anthony is a black student who saw his friend Michael beaten to death last week by a gang of white kids. Tonight Anthony sees one of the white kids, who's been arrested, on the TV news.

The Response: Anthony hates the kid on the news and the others who killed Michael. He hopes they'll suffer in hell forever.

The Responsibility:

0% Anthony's _____ 100% Anthony's

Clearing the Air

O Lord,

you have searched me and you know
me. . . Where can I go from your Spirit?
Where can I flee from your presence?. . .
Search me, O God, and know my heart;
test me and know my anxious thoughts.
See if there is any offensive way in me,
and lead me in the way everlasting.

(Psalm 139:1, 7, 23, 24)

Sin	Confess it to . . .	Restitution?	Replace it with . . .
Shoplifting			
Thinking lustful thoughts			
Making fun of a friend behind her back			

The Long Haul

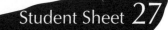

Part I:
Tips on Renewing Your Mind

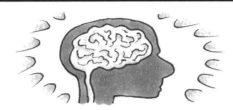

1. Spend time with God. Make prayer, Bible study, and Scripture memorization part of your life. The power of God's Word can help you change, so use it!

2. Walk in the Spirit. Each step you take to obey God in resisting temptation will make it easier to take the next step. Pretty soon, you'll have built a habit. Walking in the Spirit isn't anything mystical. It simply means when you read in the Bible something good to do or something bad to avoid, you obey. And when God brings something to mind—someone to help or a bad situation to correct—you obey. The more you obey, the more sensitive you'll become in "hearing" what God is saying to you throughout the day.

3. Keep at it. Don't give up on the process. Try looking for one step of obedience you can take each week.

4. Be accountable to someone else. Get a friend to run the race with you.

Part II:
Keeping Tabs

Here are a few pointers to help you develop a friendship for spiritual accountability:

1. Meet with someone of the same sex. You probably can be more open and honest about all your temptations this way.

2. Meet with the same person. Don't bounce from person to person. Keep meeting with the same person to build a consistent relationship.

3. Meet regularly and consistently. Find a time that you can meet once every week at the same place and time if possible. Leave room for flexibility, though. If you need to change the time, day, or place for one or more meetings, go ahead.

4. Talk about specific issues. Don't turn the time into a social session. Agree on the issues you'll talk about.

5. Hold each other accountable. Don't avoid tough subjects. Agree to be honest about what you've done during the past week.

6. Guard your conversations. Don't share your conversations with anyone else unless the other person has given you specific permission to do so. Exceptions: See #10.

7. Pray for one another. Pray about the specific issues you're facing.

8.. Memorize Scripture together. Work on learning one new verse each week. Select the same verses if you can—ones that will help you with your temptations.

9. Build the friendship under the guidance of a spiritual leader. Let your youth leader or pastor know that you're meeting, and keep him or her up to date on how it's going. Agree as a pair to talk with this leader openly about what you're working on.

10. Seek outside help if one person has a serious problem. If your partner has a question to which neither of you knows the answer, talk together with an adult. And don't keep quiet if your friend is talking about something serious like deep depression, suicide, pregnancy, or crime. Get help.